Language and Gender

- Angela Goddard and Lindsey Meân Patterson

LONDON AND NEW YORK

First published 2000
by Routledge
11 New Fetter Lane, London EC4P 4EE

Simultaneously published in the USA
and Canada
by Routledge
29 West 35th Street, New York, NY 10001

*Routledge is an imprint of the Taylor & Francis
Group*

© 2000 Angela Goddard and Lindsey
Meân Patterson

Typeset in Stone Sans/Stone Serif by
Solidus (Bristol) Limited

Printed and bound in Great Britain by
TJ International Ltd, Padstow, Cornwall

*British Library Cataloguing in Publication
Data*

A catalogue record for this book is
available from the British Library

*Library of Congress Cataloging in Publication
Data*

A catalogue record for this book has been
requested.

ISBN 0–415–20177–2

Language and Gender

This accessible satellite textbook in the Routledge INTERTEXT series is unique in offering students hands-on practical experience of textual analysis focused on language and gender. Written in a clear, user-friendly style, it combines practical activities with texts, accompanied by commentaries and suggestions for further study. It can be used individually or in conjunction with the series core textbook, *Working with Texts: A core book for language analysis.*

Aimed at A-Level and beginning undergraduate students, *Language and Gender*:

- explores the relationship between language and our ideas about men and women;
- challenges commonly expressed views on the subject of language and gender;
- highlights the individual's role in the expression of gender stereotyping;
- includes a range of text types as diverse as personal ads, wildlife documentary, literary fiction, advertisements, and classical music programmes;
- includes a comprehensive glossary of terms.

Angela Goddard is Senior Lecturer in Language at the Centre for Human Communication, Manchester Metropolitan University and was Chief Moderator for the research project element of the NEAB English Language A-Level for twelve years. **Lindsey Meân Patterson** is Senior Lecturer in Social Psychology at the Centre for Human Communication at Manchester Metropolitan University.

011

The series editors:

Ronald Carter is Professor of Modern English Language in the Department of English Studies at the University of Nottingham and is the editor of the Routledge INTERFACE series in Language and Literary Studies. He is also co-author of *The Routledge History of Literature in English*. From 1989 to 1992 he was seconded as National Director for the Language in the National Curriculum (LINC) project, directing a £21.4 million in-service teacher education programme.

Angela Goddard is Senior Lecturer in Language at the Centre for Human Communication, Manchester Metropolitan University, and was Chief Moderator for the project element of English Language A-Level for the Northern Examination and Assessment Board (NEAB) from 1983 to 1995. Her publications include *The Language Awareness Project: Language and Gender*, vols I and II, 1988, and *Researching Language*, 1993 (Framework Press).

First series title:

Working with Texts: A core book for language analysis
Ronald Carter, Angela Goddard, Danuta Reah, Keith Sanger, Maggie Bowring

Satellite titles:

The Language of Politics
Adrian Beard

The Language of Poetry
John McRae

The Language of Sport
Adrian Beard

The Language of Newspapers
Danuta Reah

The Language of Advertising: Written texts
Angela Goddard

The Language of Humour
Alison Ross

Language and Gender
Angela Goddard and Lindsey Meân Patterson

The Language of Fiction
Keith Sanger

Related titles:

INTERFACE series:

Feminist Stylistics
Sara Mills

Language, Society and Power: An Introduction
Linda Thomas and Shân Wareing

contents

Acknowledgements   vi

Introduction   1

Unit one: Projections   **5**

Unit two: Making up gender   **27**

Unit three: All in the mind?   **47**

Unit four: Political correctness   **69**

Unit five: Gender and speech styles   **85**

Unit six: Reading positions   **107**

Index of terms   115
References   119
Further reading   121

acknowledgements

Many thanks to the following for their useful comments on draft units:

Neil Carey, Centre for Human Communication, Manchester Metropolitan University. Adrian Beard and Chris Thompson, English Department, Gosforth High School, Newcastle Upon Tyne;

and to the following for foreign language data:

Julia Gillen, Centre for Human Communication, Manchester Metropolitan University.
Jean Hudson, Cambridge University Press.
Martha Jones, University of Nottingham.

The following texts and illustrations have been reprinted courtesy of their copyright holders:

1   Extract from 'Rum Punch by Leonard Elmore. Copyright © 1992 by Elmore Leonard. Used by permission of Delacorte Press, a division of Random House, Inc.
2   'The big C: Joan Smith asks why all the fuss over one little four-letter word' by Joan Smith. First published in *The Guardian*, G2, p. 5, 3 March 1998. Copyright © 1998 Joan Smith.
3   Argos Plus flyer and computer feature used by permission of Argos.
4   British Gas advertisement used by permission of British Gas.
5   Jak cartoons used by permission of the *Evening Standard*/Solo Syndication.
6   Extract from *Seduction* by Charlotte Lamb by permission of Harlequin Books S.A. First published by Mills and Boon® in Great Britain in 1980. Copyright © by Charlotte Lamb 1980.
7   'Men Talk' from *Dreaming Frankenstein* (1986) by Liz Lochhead is reprinted by permission of Polygon.
8   FAT FREDDY'S CAT, copyright © and ™ Gilbert Shelton, 1999.
9   LOST CONSONANT No. 33, 'One of man's earliest inventions was the heel' by Graham Rawle reproduced by permission of The Agency (London) Ltd © Graham Rawle 1991.
10 3-Star Skincare advertisement used by permission of Aramis.
11 Stonemarket catalogue 'cock and hen stone image' image used by permission of Stonemarket Ltd, Warwickshire.
12 Independent masthead and headline used by permission of *The Independent*.
13 Lloyds TSB logo used by permission of Lloyds TSB Bank plc.
14 Lynx logo used by permission of Lynx Express.

While the authors and the publishers have made every effort to contact copyright holders of the material used in this volume, they would be happy to hear from anyone they were unable to contact.

introduction

This is a small book about a big area. The aim of this Introduction is to explain the rationale for the selection of material, and to clarify the meaning of certain important terms.

Sex and gender

First, the title. *Language and Gender* refers to the relationship between language and our ideas about men and women. 'Gender' as a term differs from 'sex' in being about socially expected characteristics rather than biology. So, for instance, while possessing different genitalia is about biological factors, seeing this as leading to certain forms of behaviour is about gender.

One example of this process is the traditional idea in medicine and early psychology that people with wombs were more likely to be emotionally unstable. We can see this connection in the origin of the terms 'hysteria' and 'hysterical', which come from the Greek *husterikos*, meaning 'of the womb'. Hysterical behaviour has traditionally been associated with women, and their biology has been given as the 'cause'. In this case as in many others, biology has been used to justify our social judgements, but this version of biology is itself socially constructed.

You may tell yourself that this is all distant history, and that because there is no obvious biological reference in the term 'hysterical', there is no issue to discuss here. But would you even now describe a man as being 'hysterical'? If not, is that because men don't behave in that way, or is it because this same behaviour in men would be called something else, perhaps something more positive?

Man, male, masculine

While the terms 'man' and 'woman' can refer to definitions based on biological differences, the terms 'masculine' and 'feminine' are always about expected gender characteristics – what men and women are supposed to be like. The 'ine' ending itself means 'like', as in 'bovine' (like a cow), 'vulpine' (like a wolf), 'Geraldine' (like a Gerald). (No, that last example wasn't a mistake.)

While 'man' and 'woman' are nouns and therefore suggest 'people', 'masculine' and 'feminine' are adjectives and suggest qualities or attributes. So we could talk about 'masculine women' and 'feminine men' and be thinking about people who depart from the norm of what we consider appropriate for each sex. There is a third pair of terms – 'male' and 'female' – that can and often do shift between positions, according to the writer's intentions. If people talk about 'males' and 'females', they could be using the terms as nouns, as alternatives to 'men' and 'women'; but these terms can also function as adjectives, like 'masculine' and 'feminine'. So a writer might be talking of 'male behaviour' and really mean 'masculine behaviour'.

If you are going to get to grips with the ideas above, you need to do some practical investigating. As is true of all the satellite texts in the *Intertext* series, this book aims to give you some starting points for research of your own. But the topic of language and gender is a bit different from others in this series, in that there is already much published material on it, aimed at different age groups and operating at different levels. In particular, many textbooks aimed at secondary age students cover the idea of sexism in language and images, especially in the mass media. It is therefore likely that you will have 'done' this topic, perhaps several times, over the course of your school/college career. So why do it all over again in this book?

It isn't the case that just because you've 'done' gender as a topic, that there's nothing else to say. For a start, you need to ask *how* you studied this topic: what were the assumptions behind the thinking you were given, and that you yourself did? Also, research in this area has changed considerably over the years: how do you know that you're not stuck in the 1970s?

The comments below will outline the particular focus we have taken in helping you to get a perspective on what you might already have studied.

'The English language is sexist.'
'Sex stereotyping is all the fault of the media and of society.'
'Women use powerless language and that makes them inferior.'

These extracts from student essays show some commonly expressed ideas, and ideas that we want to challenge in this book in the following ways:

◎ people often put the blame for stereotyping elsewhere – for example, it's in the language itself, it's the fault of the media, it's to do with 'society'. They tend not to include themselves in their account. Our aim is to show how we all 'do' gender in our everyday thinking;

◎ looking at everyday thinking means looking at psychological processes and at social organisation. It's not enough just to look at language without considering how it relates to wider issues about how we think and understand, and how we view our own and others' social groups. So, for example, saying that a particular term is 'stereotyped' doesn't get us very far without some exploration of what the process of stereotyping might be about;

◎ there are many books on the subject of the linguistic usages of men and women, particularly on the differences between them. But the very fact that there is a lot of research causes a problem: how can you assess where any one article or textbook stands in the history of research in this area? For example, current ideas about 'powerless language' are certainly not those described above. So, rather than offering a catalogue of 'differences' - which you can easily get from elsewhere if you want them - we are offering ways for you to think about any account of 'difference' that you may read.

Because of the nature of what we are trying to do, you may well find that this book varies in how interactively it works: there are many activities, but there are also some sections that ask you to read blocks of text and think. So be prepared for some variation.

3

Projections

The aim of this unit is to get you thinking about the relationship between the language we use and the world around us. Consideration of this is important when looking at language and gender, because we need to establish how far our ideas about the sexes are the result of seeing what we want to see - or, rather, seeing what we *have* to see because of the language that is available to us.

The Sapir-Whorf hypothesis

The issue of whether language is simply a direct reflection of the world around us has been debated for many centuries. For example, the Ancient Greek philosopher, Socrates, asked questions about whether there was any intrinsic connection between an object and its name. In more recent times, the linguist, Edward Sapir, and the psychologist, Benjamin Lee Whorf, found themselves asking questions in the same broad area of language and thought as a result of their anthropological work with speakers of different languages, particularly North American Indian languages. They concluded that we are not simply passive recorders of what we find around us in language; rather, we impose our ideas on our environment as a result of the language we have.

This is how they put this concept, which has come to be termed 'The Sapir-Whorf hypothesis':

> We dissect nature along lines laid down by our native languages.
> The categories and types that we isolate from the world of phe-
> nomena we do not find there because they stare every observer
> in the face; on the contrary, the world is presented in a kal-
> eidoscopic flux of impressions which has to be organized by our
> minds - and this means largely by the linguistic systems in our
> minds
>
> (Whorf, 1956: 213)

In other words, when we acquire language, we acquire ways of thinking -
conceptual systems or grids - which we don't notice consciously because
they just feel natural to us. It's a bit like viewing the world through a
particular pair of spectacles that we've got used to wearing. And these
spectacles are our culture. Some speakers - bilingual language users, for
example - have more than one pair of spectacles. And here, speakers
readily attest to the fact that they think differently when they use their
different languages. Professional interpreters spend their working lives
trying to match a set of concepts from one language with the words of
another. And sometimes, there are gaps where an idea in one language is
simply not encoded in another. For example, in Russian, there are no
words to label 'hand' or 'foot' as separate from the arm or leg. Examples
such as these give us evidence of the existence of the Sapir-Whorf
'linguistic systems' mentioned above.

Further practical examples of different languages encoding 'reality'
differently are not hard to find. One of the most commonly quoted areas
is colour terms. English, for example, has 11 basic words for colours -
white, black, red, green, yellow, blue, brown, purple, pink, orange and
grey. (This list does not include terms for colours that are incorporated in
other colours - for example, beige is a form of brown, sage is a form of
green, and so on.) In contrast, speakers of some New Guinea Highland
languages have only two terms: 'dark' and 'light'. It's clear that in labelling
colours, speakers of different languages chop up the spectrum in different
ways - as below, where some English and Welsh terms are mapped against
each other. What's harder to determine is whether this means the
speakers of different languages actually see differently when they look at
the same colour.

Another aspect of describing colour which appears to vary on a
language basis is **metaphorical** reference. For example, where English
speakers talk of 'blue jokes', in Spanish these are 'green' (but in
Mexican Spanish, 'red' (Jones, 1999)); while 'green' for English speakers
has at least two sets of **connotations**: ecologically-minded, and un-
practised (with the suggestion of naïvety). English has many negative

Text: Colour terms map

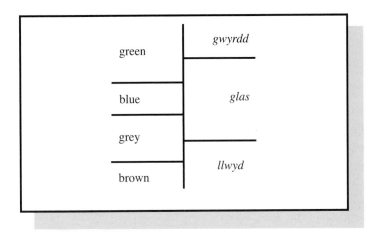

connotations for the term 'black', which many people have seen as the cultural legacy of a white-dominated society. Black is used for bereavement, in contrast to the white clothes people wear to funerals in India. In English, white often stands for purity, while red connotes danger (or anger, as in 'seeing red') and yellow connotes cowardice. The list is long but that doesn't mean there's any logic in any of the relationships between the colour terms and the ideas that they call up for any group of speakers. These meanings are **arbitrary**: if we have associations for a particular colour term, it's more likely to be because we put them there than because they occurred somehow 'naturally'. If they occurred naturally, then everyone would have the same system.

The way speakers establish categories in language can be shown to relate to what they need language for - in other words, what the pre-occupations are in their particular community. Frequently discussed examples of this are that Inuit people have different words for snow, nomadic Arabic groups many words for different types of camel, and Australian aboriginal languages many words for different types of hole in the sand. Different lifestyles mean that some groups need to pay more attention than others to particular aspects of the environment, leading to more or less fine **discriminations** within language categories. These discriminations are important for the members of the community in question: a mistake about the weight that a patch of snow can carry, about the value of a camel, or about the type of creature that may inhabit a hole in the sand, all have real-life consequences. Snow, camels and sand-holes all have 'reality', but the fine distinctions between the various different types are unlikely to be noticed by outsiders, for whom variations are not significant, or **salient**. If variations are noticed, they will be seen as minor variations that can easily be accommodated by the single terms they already have: to people from a temperate climate, snow is just snow, whatever its condition.

But languages don't only differ in the names they have for objects. They also differ in how they organise abstract ideas, such as ways of talking about relationships, or the qualities that people have. And here the possible effects of language upon thought seem more significant. For we are talking about our social values, how we treat each other and organise ourselves within society. However, abstract ideas are more elusive to grasp than the names of objects, and their effects are more difficult to plot.

Activity

As a brief initial exploration of the Sapir–Whorf hypothesis, consider the following:

Swedish speakers have a term – *sambo* (*bo* = 'live', pronounced 'boo') – for a person they are living with but not married to. They also have the further terms below for people they are involved with:

> *sarbo* to refer to a partner who does not live with the speaker;
> *narbo* to refer to a partner who lives close to the speaker – e.g. a few streets away;
> *delsbo* (*dels* = 'partly') to refer to a partner who has a house of their own, but with whom the speaker lives for part of the time.

None of these terms are marked for the sex of the person who is being referred to (Hudson, 1999).

In English, we can refer to a person we are having a love relationship with in at least the following ways:

> my lover;
> my partner;
> my girlfriend/my boyfriend;
> my friend.

1   Can you add any further terms you use to the English list?
2   If you speak another language, what are the choices in that language?
3   Are you happy with the terms you can choose from, or do you think there are gaps? If there are gaps, what is it that you cannot express satisfactorily?
4   To what extent do the English terms force you to specify the sex of the person you are involved with?
5   Do you think that different groups in society might use the terms on the list in different ways? For example, how might a speaker's age or sexual orientation affect their choices and intended meanings?
6   What ideas are encoded by the Swedish terms? Would you find the Swedish categories useful? What might their existence within the Swedish system suggest about Swedish culture?

Commentary

The responses you gathered to the questions above are likely to have varied according to a number of factors. The notes here are just an indication of some of the possible variables. One piece of recent research (Harvey, 1997) which surveyed usage among straight and gay male users of English found that age was significant for straight men in that the term 'girlfriend' suggested youth. Beyond that, the term 'partner' was seen by straight men as suggesting permanence and seriousness of relationship, while 'lover' suggested something less serious. However, gay men had different readings for some of the terms. For example, gay men saw the term 'boyfriend' as giving a more long-term, serious message about the relationship (regardless of the age factor) than 'lover'. Many of the gay interviewees commented that the term they chose would very much depend on who they were talking to and what environment they were in.

This activity was designed to get you thinking about the available options in any one language system. Aside from the way in which different languages present different options, however, it is important to realise that there are different groups within the same language system who might be served more or less well by the options available.

A broad point to make about the language choices presented here is that choices are clearly subject to change. For example, the term 'partner' is a relatively new phenomenon. This means that the Sapir–Whorf hypothesis cannot be true in any extreme way, otherwise language change of this kind would never be possible. New social practices and configurations — in this case, people deciding to live together rather than get married — cause new language to emerge. But the fact that people want their experiences to be named at all should tell us something about the role of language, which is clearly to validate and legitimise a person's behaviour. The feeling that a word lends a sense of reality to an idea proves how powerful language is in our reading of the world.

Anthropomorphism

Anthropomorphism means 'giving something a human shape', and describes another kind of projection that we often see in language. Exploration of this area will provide some more exemplification of the relationship between language and thought.

Perhaps human beings are essentially very lonely and insecure creatures. For it seems that we need to constantly project the idea of humanness onto the inanimate world. We make cartoons for children where objects like brooms and spoons talk and sing; one of our most successful credit card adverts in the 1980s featured a nervous Cockney-speaking pound sign called Money and his confident flexible friend, Access; we give our cars affectionate names and even call death-making bombs and hurricanes after human beings. Perhaps we hope that if we can humanise the inanimate world, it will seem friendlier and therefore less terrifying. The persuasive potential of this anthropomorphism is not lost on advertisers: see the advert on the next page.

As well as giving animacy to inanimate objects, we also 'humanise' the animal kingdom, often giving characteristics to animals that are completely unrelated to their behaviour in their natural habitat. For example, no one who has ever observed wild bears would think of them as the cuddly, soft items that populate the current 'Teddy Bear' shops.

10

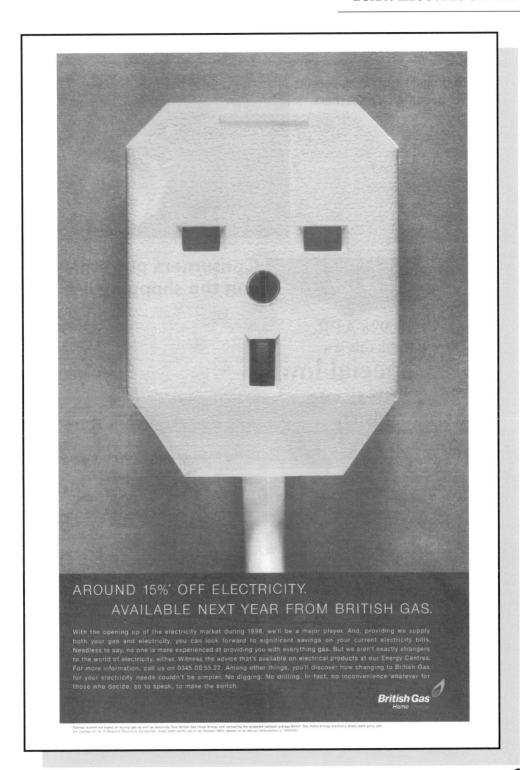

Activities

Below are some advertising logos featuring animals. The company using each logo is listed below. Why do you think the companies chose each of these symbols? What connotations are they hoping to suggest?

a) Swan (kitchen appliances)
b) Lloyds TSB Bank
c) Lynx (parcel delivery service)

Text: Animal icons

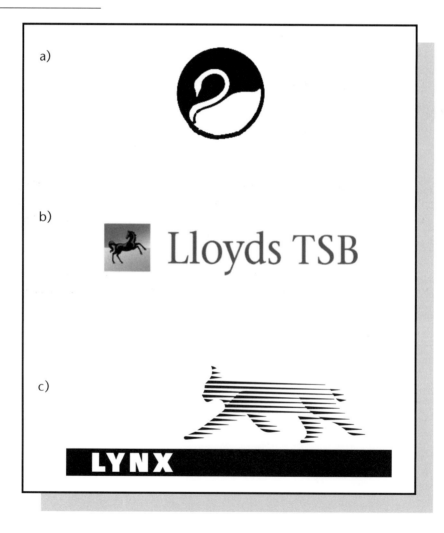

◎   What characteristics do we ascribe to the animals in the following list?

◎   To what extent are these characteristics projections by humans onto the animals?

◎   Can you think of any other animals that we describe in particular ways?

snake	fox	lamb
slug	wolf	owl
shark	pig	rat
cat	dog	worm

What do we mean when we say the following about humans?

He/she is . . .

a snake	a rat
a fox	a cat
a lamb	a pussycat
a slug	a tiger
a wolf	a dog
a shark	a worm
a pig	a mouse

Do the animal names above vary according to the sex of the person being referred to? For example, are some used more often to describe one sex than the other? Are some used for both sexes, but mean something different when used about one sex or the other?

In the Boots Christmas catalogue on p. 14, why do you think the products aimed at men use these particular animals? How does the verbal language that accompanies the images reinforce the messages given?

Text: Boots catalogue

Text: Fat Freddy's cat

'God bless her, and all who sail in her'

So far, we have looked at the way we project human qualities onto both inanimate objects and animals. But, as the previous activity suggested, we also project gender. The title above is part of a well-known ritual whereby a ship is launched and blessed. But why is it not: 'God bless it, and all who sail in it'? Or even: 'God bless him, and all who sail in him'?

Some commentators (for example, Spender, 1980) have suggested that cars, as well as boats, are seen as female because they are objects of status that have traditionally been under the control of men. Certainly, the physical attractiveness of such objects is often at the forefront of descriptions, in the same way as women are often described in terms of their looks. For example, here is an extract from a news report on the de-commissioning of the Royal Yacht *Britannia*:

> 'a ship which has given good faithful service for 44 years, and which is still as elegant now as when she was commissioned...'.
>
> (Radio 4 *News*, 12 noon, 10/12/97)

If Spender is right about why some objects are personified as female, it doesn't follow that it's only men who use language in this way, nor does it mean that every usage of this kind is a conscious one. Spender is talking about a male perspective, or way of viewing the world, that is encoded in the language we all use as a common resource. And it is precisely because we use language without analysing each and every item that a way of thinking can exist without really being noticed. It is only when our flow of language is disrupted that we become conscious of the thinking that is embedded in language – and then we can ask whose thinking it really is. Here is an example of that process in action. The news journalist, Sue McGregor, in covering a world energy conference, is talking to another journalist about Britain's past record on industrial pollution:

> 'but Britain's been a good boy, hasn't she ... or he?' (*nervous laughter*)
>
> (*Today* Programme, Radio 4, 9/12/97)

Sue McGregor finds it difficult to continue her presentation of Britain as a 'good boy' because as soon as a **pronoun reference** is needed, 'she' emerges automatically, causing the journalist some confusion and embarrassment. It appears that as far as pronouns are concerned, our ideas about the gender of, not just mechanical objects, but also countries, are deeply embedded in our thinking. Countries are so often depicted as female, as in the headline below:

Text: *Independent* headline

THE INDEPENDENT

Thursday 23 October 1997   45p   No 3,435 ••••

America reveals her policy on global warming: too little, too late

that if the headline had read:

> AMERICA REVEALS HIS POLICY ON GLOBAL WARMING: TOO LITTLE, TOO LATE

then it would seem as though America was revealing the policy of a male individual (perhaps the President?). In other words, the 'his' would not appear connected to 'America' at all.

Countries do not always appear as 'she', however. For example, during the period of Fascist rule in Germany leading up to World War II, Germany was often referred to in Fascist literature as the 'Fatherland'. But it's interesting to note the link between the idea of Germany as male and the qualities that were being stressed - not Germany's ability to feed and nurture its people, but the military might of the country, its readiness for adversity. Pronoun usage therefore appears to be part of a larger picture where we use notions of male and female to stand for different sets of qualities. The pages that follow will explore this is more detail, as will the next unit.

Mother Nature, Father Time

The use of 'she' to refer to a country often appears to go along with the idea of a matriarchal figure originating and sustaining its people (as in 'mother country' and 'mother tongue'). This idea is also encoded in the idea of 'Mother Nature', a nurturing, protecting force. In a popular children's cartoon, 'SuperTed', the teddy bear figure, initially a factory

17

reject, is claimed by Mother Nature and given superpowers to fight wrong-doing. Mother Nature, with her friendly wand, here resembles a fairy godmother, a very different figure from that traditionally associated with 'Father Time', who is often pictured as stern, authoritarian and inhumane:

> Time hath, my lord, a wallet at his back,
> Wherein he puts alms for oblivion,
> A great-sized monster of ingratitudes:
> Those scraps are good deeds past; which are devoured
> As fast as they are made, forgot as soon
> As done.
>
> (Shakespeare, *Troilus and Cressida*, Act III, iii: 145–50)

Sometimes, gender projections onto the inanimate world appear to encode qualities which are polar opposites. They occur in a wide range of different domains, from the kind of visual **metonymy** represented by the 'cock' and 'hen' stones on p. 19, which represent the idea of high and low, respectively, to the aural differences represented by the 'male' and 'female' endings of poetry lines. The male ending (also called a 'strong' ending) represents a stressed syllable at the end of the line, while a female ending (also called a 'weak' ending) has an unstressed syllable. This is exemplified below, where the first and third lines have feminine endings, and the rest, masculine endings:

> 'Tis Spring, come out to ramble (F)
> The hilly brakes around, (M)
> For under thorn and bramble (F)
> About the hollow ground (M)
> The primroses are found. (M)
>
> (A.E. Housman, 'The Lent Lily', in Horwood 1971)

Text: Garden catalogue

On p. 20 is an extract from a music programme, written to accompany a performance of classical music. Each paragraph has been numbered for easy reference.

There are no pronouns used to describe the musical instruments, but they are anthropomorphised in various ways. Plot the way the text works, paying particular attention to how the instruments are seen in terms of gender. It may be useful for you to know that the story the music is based on is that of two lovers, Tristan (male) and Isolde (female).

Start by answering these specific questions:

1   Which instruments are seen as masculine? Which are seen as feminine?
2   Which themes (used in the passage to mean 'recurring parts of the music') are seen as masculine, and which as feminine?
3   Which words in the passage give us clues to what the writer means by 'masculine' and 'feminine'?
4   Are there any other ways in which human social values and judgements are being projected onto this account of music? For example, is race indicated in any way?

Music programme issued at the Bridgewater Hall, Manchester for a performance of Messiaen's *Turangalila* on Sunday, 22nd September, 1996

Introduction

1 The *Introduction* is a kind of preface to the symphony, a clear though by no means dispassionate presentation of the two basic themes and some of the major protagonists. From the emotional point of view, the most significant of the protagonists are the piano, which has a heroic solo part, and the Ondes Martenot, an electronic instrument which though primitive by modern standards (it was invented as long as 65 years ago by Maurice Martenot) has a voice and character all its own. The piano part was written for Yvonne Loriod, one of Messiaen's composition pupils whom he later married, and the Ondes Martenot part for her sister, Jeanne Loriod.

2 It is not insignificant that the piano and the Ondes make their first entry at the same time as that of the first main theme, not with the theme itself but in shrieks and tremolandos as trombones and tuba stride in with their symbol of monumental masculinity. It is not too fanciful either to describe the second main theme, which appears very briefly and very quietly on two clarinets, as feminine: Messiaen himself defines it as a 'flower' theme.

Chant d'amour I

3 The third main theme of the symphony, the love theme, does not make a full and definitive appearance until the sixth movement. In the recurring sections Tristan is represented by a vigorous and passionate trumpet tune based on the masculine theme from the first movement; Isolde is represented by a suddenly slow and tender melody, which is partly an echo of the feminine theme and partly an anticipation of the love theme, characteristically coloured by Ondes Martenot and upper strings in octaves. The Isolde theme makes a climactic reappearance before the end of the movement.

Jardin du sommeil d'amour

4 The two central movements are both tertiary constructions and, in that they represent two different aspects of the consummation of the love of Tristan and Isolde, they can be taken together. *Joie du sang des étoiles* ('Joy of the blood of the stars') has been described by Messiaen as an 'African dance' which, applied to this unbridled expression of physical joy, is surely an understatement. It is based exclusively on the masculine

motif – first in a vigorous, thrusting version greeted by shrieks from the Ondes Martnenot; then in several transformations as rhythmic characters in the middle section; and finally, after an explosive piano cadenza at the climax of the movement, in a massive augmentation for the whole orchestra.

Commentary

This description of music represents masculinity in terms of size and volume ('monumental'), energetic movement ('stride in', 'vigorous', 'thrusting'), and expansive feeling ('passionate'). It is represented by loud brass instruments such as trombone, tuba, and trumpet. In contrast, femininity is seen as quiet, slow, tender and delicate (flower-like), expressed by piano, Ondes (a piano-like instrument), strings and clarinet. The 'female' instruments are often reactive, responding to the 'male' ones with shrieks and trembling notes. African culture is associated with physicality of an animal ('unbridled') kind.

This picture resembles the very sex-typed roles found in traditional romantic stories, such as those of Mills and Boon, particularly in the idea of active masculine sexuality and female passivity. The idea of African figures as non-civilised and close to 'nature' features in many texts – for example, in advertisements that want to associate their product with ideas of physical strength, exoticness or untamed wildness. When was the last time you saw an African figure representing intellectual prowess or capitalistic success in adverts for computer software or business class travel?

The sex life of seals

Natural history programmes are useful sources of evidence for investi-gating anthropomorphism and, within this, projections of gender. Such programmes are particularly important because they are often cited as proof that human beings are, or should be, 'naturally' disposed to behave in a certain way. The argument goes: look, the animals, our relatives, do it this way, so it must be only natural for us to do so.

But the question is, do the human observers record objectively what they see, or do they project onto the animal world aspects of human behaviour, with all our attached ideas of relationships between male and female human beings?

21

Academics who have researched the way wildlife programmes are presented (for example, Coward (1984), and Crowther and Leith (1995), claim that such programmes involve humans projecting onto the animal world aspects of human behaviour, which they then 'find' there and claim as evidence for a natural order. A further claim is that such presentations consist overwhelmingly of male scientists talking to each other and presenting their stories about animals from the perspective of the male animals they are observing.

Activity

The following is an extract from the Radio 4 *Natural History Programme*, 7 December 1997.

The presenter (A) travels to a remote Scottish island called North Rona to meet a researcher (B) who is studying grey seals. Both A and B are male.

◎ To what extent are the human speakers anthropomorphising the animals they are talking about? Can you find examples of language that might be more appropriate to describe human relationships than those of animals?

◎ How are the male and female animals presented in the programme?

◎ Is the account presented from the point of view of male, or female, animals? How might the account have differed if it had taken the point of view of another group?

A: ... But anyway, it's grey seals that we're here to see and, er, I'm gonna drop down on the cliff now and meet [name of researcher] of [name of university] a researcher there, and he works specifically on the male grey seal. We're sitting in a sea of seals and, er, all looking like huge great maggots on this great big glassy slope and in fact two are fighting right in front of us.

B: Oh, that's not actually a fight, that's sex really, believe it or not. That's the dominant male for this, er, group of females that we're, er, sitting above here and, er, he's basically showing his passions for her, basically. The average duration of copulation is about twenty minutes but they can actually last up to well over an hour. I think the longest one I've observed is sixty-five minutes. I think that's basically as long as the male needs to mate with a female to actually inseminate her.

A: The odd cry, the odd huge snort with masses of mucus flying out of their nostrils, about sort of two yards. Well, listen to him, he, he growls rather like a bear. Bears might be quite a good way to describe them because they're actually very hairy, aren't they?

B: They are. In many ways their behavioural postures even though they've got very short flippers are very bear-like or at least dog-like anyway.

A: Oh he charged him – a great big growl, a great snap at the back of his hind flippers.

B: Yeah, they don't like being bitten round the hind flippers, that's where they're very vulnerable.

A: And you can hear him sort of flopping along like a great big sort of caterpillar. Well, just to paint a picture for everybody 'cos it really is amazing, what we're looking at. There must be three or four hundred animals, goodness knows how many in front of us and of the animals that we can see, we can see lots are obviously pups, those gorgeous white velvety animals with huge great big dishy eyes, and um, lots of mottled coloured animals which are much bigger and, they're the females, and considerably fewer but much larger animals, these great big sort of warriors, the bulls.

B: That's it, the sex ratio of adult females to adult males on the breeding colony is about one male to seven females and the males will stay here for up to eight or nine weeks at a time without feeding but relying on their blubber reserves and trying to mate with as many females as possible.

A: And even as a lay person looking at these animals I can see that there's a male surrounded by several females and that pattern is repeated across the whole of this hillside right down to the sea.

B: It is effectively a polygamous system, each of the successful males will probably mate with ten to twelve females during the breeding season. There's a lot of males that don't manage to get any copulations at all, but it's very different strategies that the males employ such as these resident males we see before us sitting amongst their groups of females, they're very socially dominant – they will chase off other males and engage in aggressive interactions.

A: We've seen lots of fights, haven't we? I mean, these fights are posturing. I mean they draw blood, but they are vicious, aren't they?

B: The really vicious fights tend to be between neighbouring resident males because they're very equally matched and when they eventually do come to blows they are fairly severe fights.

A: They're like real warriors if they, if they win over that ... I mean, they posture right up, don't they; 'I'm the winner of this one!'

B: They quite often roll on their back and wave their foreflippers in the air, as well as a sort of a victory gesture.

A: And this male mating right in front of us now, he's a warrior, he's a successful male.

B: He's been here right from the start of the season and he's doing very well already - he's had six copulations that I've observed anyway. But you'll notice occasionally other males - there is one over here which is, you may have more difficulty in distinguishing him from a female.

A: Yes, he looks very like a female. I mean he's actually really low down on the grass, he's kind of rather roman-nosed, sort of bent over contours of the tussock grass.

B: Indeed, he's, er, much smaller and sleeker and as you notice he's not got much scarring on him. Ah this male strategy is very different - he'll basically sneak around almost pretending to be a female and er ...

A: Warrior in a girl's blouse.

B: Yeah, and he'll keep out of the way of trouble and if one of the resident males comes towards him to threaten him, he'll just run away, he'll bolt and hide somewhere and then when the resident male disappears again to go and check out some female he'll sneak back in again and just lie down and wait and when you watch one of these more peripheral males trying to mate with a female there's often far more aggression from the female, they'll really object to that mating. In some cases it almost amounts to a rape, the male forces a copulation on the female.

A: Why does he do that? I mean, he doesn't have to engage in fights. I can see the advantage there but he picks up a huge resistance from the females and these females are no mean match, I mean, they are big and they've got lots of teeth, they could inflict a lot of damage I would have thought.

B: That's true, but there's also a cost to being a resident male. As I said, these resident males will stay for the whole breeding season, they lose about two kilograms of weight a day, relying on their blubber reserves. They're not feeding and towards the end of the season you see these resident males and they're basically just a bag of bones, basically, and they're scarred and bloodied from the encounters with their neighbouring resident males.

A: I see, so these peripheral males are cheats, really.

B: They run around a lot, they're very active and mobile but they avoid the serious fights from the males, they get more aggression from the females, certainly.

A: And are they always cheaters, or do they turn into warriors?

B: Well, that's an interesting question, we've got one friend just up the slope here and he's been here since 1987, my first year out here, and he started out as one of these runaround males and he graduated slowly into a more resident male and this year he's holding himself a nice position amongst a good group of females and doing very well.

Summary

This unit has suggested that language is not a neutral reflection of the world around us, but that, by using language, we project onto the world our own sense of 'reality'. Starting with the idea that different languages encode objects and ideas differently, we then went on to look at two specific types of projection: the projection of humanness onto the inanimate world; the projection of gender onto the inanimate and animal worlds. The next unit will explore further the idea of the different qualities that are seen as the appropriate domain of one sex or the other.

Extension

1   Research all the terms in the English language using 'black' and 'white': for example, 'a black look', a 'white lie'. To what extent do terms using black and white encode negative and positive meanings?

2   Make a list of all the colours that are used in English metaphorically: for example, 'I'm feeling blue' to mean 'I'm feeling depressed'. Then research the way one other language uses different colour terms metaphorically. If you are familiar with another language yourself, you could go on to consider some further areas of English and your other language where you feel there are differences in how ideas are expressed.

3   Research the use of relationship terms (lover, boyfriend, etc.). Pay attention to the idea that different groups may have different readings of the terms, and therefore different usage patterns for them.

4   Collect as many logos as you can find that use animal images. What qualities are being projected onto the animals concerned?

5   a) What animals are used to construct fantasy figures within our popular cultural stories? (For example, fairy stories, horror films, comic heroes/heroines).

b) What animal names are used to construct terms of abuse by each sex about the other?

c) What animal names are used as address terms and reference items in lovers' messages to each other? (For example, in Valentine's messages in newspapers.)

From answering the questions above, what do you conclude about the way human beings categorise animals and use them within our own referencing system? What human feelings and attitudes are evident, both about the animals and about ourselves?

6   Record and transcribe a natural history programme from the TV or radio, and consider some of the questions that were explored in this unit about anthropomorphism and projections of gender. In particular, you might ask:

a) What sex are the presenters and experts?

b) What aspects of animal behaviour are the focus of the programme? Why do you think these aspects have been selected?

c) What evidence is there that the animals are being described in anthropomorphic ways?

d) Is the account being presented from the point of view of male animals, female animals, or both?

Making up gender

The previous unit emphasised the way we project animacy and gender onto the world around us. In this unit, we will be looking at the qualities and characteristics we associate with men and women. We will do this by looking at the language we use to describe the sexes, and asking how far this language is a reflection of our learned beliefs.

This unit is called 'making up gender' for at least two reasons: one is to question whether the way we view the sexes is in any sense 'natural'; another is to suggest that we 'make up' gender as we go along. This means that, far from being a fixed and unalterable dimension that is imposed on us from on high, gender is something that we do every day as part of our social behaviour.

Bodies of description

In school, we are taught that adjectives describe items and nouns name or label them. As usual, such apparent simplicities disguise quite a lot of complexity. For a start, adjectives operate at a number of different levels. For example, the dictionary definition of a word - its **denotation** - is hardly ever the end of the story. A very potent aspect of meaning is the level of connotation a word can call up - all the associated ideas we connect with a term. Connotation is a fluid aspect of meaning, as it will depend, not only on the experiences that individuals and groups bring to interactions, but also on who is using the terms and how they are being deployed.

Activity

As an illustration of the potential differences between denotation and connotation, consider the word 'bald'. The dictionary definition of this term is 'having the scalp wholly or partly hairless'. Is that the total meaning of this word?

Brainstorm all the connotations of the adjective 'bald'. For example, are there different connotations of this term according to the type of person you picture? Does the term mean the same when applied to, say, a young man who has shaved his head, compared with an older man who is losing his hair and combs his remaining hair across the top of his head?

As well as one adjective having connotations that are very different from its denotative meaning, there are also pairs of adjectives that have the same denotation but very different connotations. For example, 'someone without children' could be the denotation of both the terms 'childless' and 'childfree', but these terms have nothing in common at the connotative level of meaning.

Just as adjectives can operate at different levels of description, so can nouns. Nouns are traditionally not thought of as descriptors; they are seen as labelling words, with the implication that things exist prior to their needing a name. At the simplest level, it is true that one of the functions of language is to name and itemise the world around us: tables, chairs and computers need to be called something. But when you get away from concrete objects, naming isn't quite so cut and dried. For example, here are two common nouns that refer to people:

bachelor   spinster

At the level of denotation, these terms mean 'unmarried adult male' and 'unmarried adult female', respectively. However, the connotations of these two nouns go much further: while a bachelor is traditionally seen as a man who has *chosen* not to marry and who is 'playing the field', a spinster is seen as a woman who has *failed* to find a husband and who has been 'left on the shelf'. Our everyday expressions, such as those in quotation marks in the previous sentence, also reveal a lot about our hidden thinking. Men are associated with sport; women, not just with shopping, but with being saleable commodities that are, in this case, past their sell-by date.

The point being made above is that even nouns, looking for all the world like simple, clear-cut labels, are categories which often mask a whole range of implicit descriptions which are very revealing of cultural values. Implicit meanings are very powerful precisely because they are unremarkable and therefore can become part of our automatic thinking.

Implicitness in itself is not necessarily a bad thing, however: as an aspect of language use, we employ it on a daily basis to make our communication more economic than it would otherwise be. For example, we can imply a great deal about people's characteristics, qualities, moods and physical states just by selecting a particular verb + adverb combination. If a friend tells you that they are *swotting frantically* for an exam, this might conjure up a picture of someone in a state of nervous exhaustion, feeling that they are running out of time, panicking, burning the midnight oil, drinking cups of black coffee to stay awake. Similarly, the choice of one particular verb over another to describe an action constructs a picture of the person being described. For example, even without the adverb 'frantically', if your friend said they were *revising* instead of swotting, or *reviewing* their work, your picture would be likely to be one of considerably more calm control.

Such language choices enable us to be economic because a lot can be left unsaid: the speaker or writer knows that the listener/reader can fill in the gaps as a result of the thinking that is shared by members of cultural groups who speak the same language.

Activity

Listed below on the left are some verb and adverb combinations for the verbs 'to run' and 'to eat'. Listed below on the right are alternative verbs. What sort of physical characteristics, personality characteristics and emotional states are implied by the descriptions?

Category	Verb + adverb	Variant verb
to run	she ran merrily, she ran jauntily, she ran slowly, she ran doggedly, she ran jerkily, she ran gracefully, she ran crazily	she pelted, she raced, she legged it, she sped, she jogged, she skipped, she ambled, she lumbered, she gambolled
to eat	he ate sloppily, he ate voraciously, he ate greedily, he ate thoughtfully, he ate warily, he ate daintily, he ate noisily, he ate carefully	he stuffed (himself), he pigged out, he savoured, he gorged, he picked at his food, he played with his food, he slurped, he nibbled, he gobbled, he dined, he supped, he chomped

29

Commentary

The descriptions above often suggest quite clear pictures of physical movement. For example, when you thought about the phrase 'she ran jerkily' you probably pictured a female figure throwing out her arms at odd angles, perhaps running at tangents rather than in a straight line. But after establishing a physical picture, a sense of the runner's state of mind also suggests itself: why is she running jerkily? What has happened to her, and what is she feeling? Some of the other examples above take us more directly to a psychological state: 'she ran doggedly' perhaps says more about the runner's determination and perseverance than her physical behaviour, attitude rather than running style.

Notice that in the second sentence of the paragraph above, it says 'you probably pictured a *female* figure . . .'. Another aspect of the way you made sense of the verbal language above was to picture the person who was performing the actions as either male or female. You were told to do this by the language of the examples: 'she' was doing all the running, 'he' was doing all the eating. You may have felt, though, that this unspecified male and female weren't always behaving as you might expect, as some terms tend to be used more about one sex than the other. For example, are 'he ate daintily', and 'he nibbled' typical phrases to describe a man? What about 'she legged it', to describe the actions of a woman, compared with 'she skipped'? Would it be a different kind of woman who would 'leg it', compared with one who would 'skip'? Would 'he skipped' be likely to occur in descriptions of an adult male? If so, what kind of man would be pictured?

All the questions raised above relate to the beliefs we have about the way men and women typically behave – their gender characteristics, those aspects we expect to be present as a result of being male or female. And our expectations are constantly validated by the operation of **collocation** in language use: the way in which words and phrases occur over and over again in certain predictable contexts – such as next to or near the words 'man' and 'woman', for example. The activity below explores the gender dimension of the company that words keep.

Activity

Read through the terms below and sort them into two lists, according to whether you think the terms are more commonly used with reference to men or to women. You might include a third list, where you think the terms can be used of either sex, but where the meaning changes according to which sex is being referred to. Can you detect any patterns in the types of words used to refer to one sex or the other?

tactful	athletic	emotional	ambitious	slim
dominant	pretty	elegant	aggressive	neat
independent	nurturing	intellectual	bubbly	neurotic
impassive	graceful	strong	empathic	agile
competitive	chatty	controlled	muscular	well-built
beautiful	handsome	fragile	bright	bimbo
hunk	kind	capable	gentle	buxom
physique	figure	rugged	tearful	hysterical

'slim, long-legged and beautiful'
'tall, powerful and charming'

Commentary

The terms you have been working with refer both to physical and to personality characteristics. You may have found that, in both respects, the terms that you associated with a male **referent** differed from those you more often see associated with a female referent.

In some cases, terms are exclusively used only about one sex or the other. For example, in describing men and women physically, men tend to have 'physiques' while women have 'figures'. The connotations of these two terms are very different: physique suggests physical strength and body size, while figure connotes aesthetic shapeliness and sexual attractiveness. Only men can be hunky and only women buxom, with the latter term being a very specific reference to breast size, while hunkiness is a much more general attribute. Sometimes, the same term could be used to describe both sexes, but the implications might differ: for example, 'well-built' could mean 'a well developed physique' when applied to a man, but when applied to a woman could be a **euphemism** for buxom, or even fat. One recent study of collocations for the terms 'man' and 'woman' (Herriman, 1998) based on the Cobuild corpus (a collection of language texts of all kinds, totalling 50 million words) found that words for physical attractiveness (pretty, sexy, glamorous) collocated most frequently with 'woman', while terms to describe height, abilities and personality most frequently collocated with 'man'.

Some terms can be used to suggest either physical characteristics or personality traits. For example, strength can be a psychological ability as well as a physical one: someone can be 'as strong as an ox'; they can also 'have the strength to cope'. How you interpreted this word will have made a difference to your results, as, while men are often seen as stronger than women physically, their psychological strength might be more readily disputed (although the referent for the phrase 'a strong silent type' is usually male).

31

Terms describing personality traits, such as 'chatty' or 'aggressive', can often be seen to fall into certain predictable patterns when used to describe the sexes. Research has consistently shown that people will willingly and easily identify characteristics which are typically male or female, but which have little to do with the actual attributes of real individuals. Morgan (1986: 179) notes a number of qualities which are typically associated with males and females in Western society. Males are seen as logical, rational, aggressive, exploitative, strategic, independent and competitive. Females are thought to be intuitive, emotional, submissive, empathic, spontaneous, nurturing and co-operative. Morgan summarises these as implying that man is 'a leader and decision-maker' while woman is 'a loyal supporter and follower'.

Social roles

Via language, we clearly construct the sexes as separate and possessing different characteristics. However, this is not the only way that our descriptions are gendered.

When we describe something, we often refer to its function and role: we talk of *wine* glasses and *dining* tables. The italic terms, or **modifiers**, are not just optional extra bits of information. They provide a detailed guide to the purpose of the objects: we are talking about glasses for wine as opposed to any other glasses (brandy glasses, cocktail glasses, sherry glasses, liqueur glasses) and a table for dining on (as opposed to a coffee table, a side table, an occasional table, a writing table). This kind of classification is very common in our everyday referencing system: we talk about *milk* bottles, *food* shops, *primary* schools, *train* journeys.

Activity

As well as thinking about and expressing what objects are for, we also ascribe functions and roles to men and women: what are men and women for, in society? To explore the way language can encode some of this information, look at the data below, which is from one day's edition of two newspapers – The Guardian and The Sun. The data describe how men and women were referred to in several of the news features covered in both papers.

◎ What types of information are given describing men and women?

◎ Are the types of information different and, if so, how?

◎ What functions, roles and relationships are being reported?

◎ How would you summarise the differences between the two newspapers in how they present men and women?

	Descriptions of women	Descriptions of men
The Guardian	Hilary his wife [Bill Clinton's] his wife Jane Radio and television's lad-girl [Zoe Ball] his girlfriend Anne-Sophie Vandamme, a social worker aged 24 Winnie [Mandela] Annette Hewins, aged 32 her niece, Donna Clarke, aged 29	Bill Clinton William Hague Clinton the Prime Minister Tony Blair General Olusegun Obasanjo Ralph George Algernon Percy, 12th Duke of Northumberland Sir William Macpherson, the Inquiry Chairman Fatboy Slim John Drewe, 50 artist John Myatt, 53 Lord Sainsbury Mr Mabille, a criminology student Gilles Naudet, a bank clerk aged 25 Lieutenant-General Sir Michael Jackson
The *Sun*	wife Patsy Kensit his estranged wife Jerry Hall pregnant model Luciana Morad Radio 1 DJ Zoe Ball *Holby City* star Lisa Faulkner sexy co-star Angela Griffin ex-missus Ollie	Oasis star Liam Gallagher Rolling Stone Mick Jagger, 55 Old Bailey judge Peter Cresswell John Drewe, 50 John Myatt, 53 fork-lift truck driver Stephen Parrott Robbie Williams

ex-*Eastenders* star	her popstar lover Fatboy Slim
Michelle Collins	love cheat Mick Jagger
Fergie	Tony Blair
ex-Ginger Spice Gerry	former Agricultural
Halliwell	Minister John Gummer
mum Jennifer Brigham	prisoner Chris Wright, 31
girlfriend, 12	barman John Smith
	groom Bob Hawkins
	Chief Executive Bob Ayling

Socialisation

To summarise so far, it is not difficult to find evidence for the idea that the language we use to talk about men and women is gendered. The way in which we talk about the sexes indicates that we possess a shared system of reference about traditional roles and about what is deemed masculine or feminine. First, we have sex-exclusive vocabulary, language that is used to describe *either* males *or* females (such as 'hunk' and 'buxom'). Second, we have language where the linguistic item remains the same but the meaning changes according to whether it is men or women who are being described. Examples can cover physical attributes, as in the term 'well-built', or behavioural traits, as in the term 'aggressive', which can have a positive meaning when applied to men (in sport, or in business contexts, for example) but has only a negative meaning when applied to women. Third, we present as **salient** *different* aspects of men and women (such as men as workers, women as mothers). We share an understanding about how men and women are meant to behave, and the characteristics they are meant to possess. This shared understanding is part of our **social knowledge**, that is, the framework we use to interpret the world – the understanding we have about how to operate in our environment, knowledge of the social rules that are part of our culture. This is not knowledge in the sense of facts or 'truth', but more a pragmatic awareness of how to function within society. We do not learn this knowledge explicitly, nor is it concrete and finite.

The process by which we acquire the social knowledge described above and make it part of the way we think is called **socialisation**. This process is extensive and includes all the things we see and hear from society around us – the people we meet, the things we're told, the images we see, the books we read, and so on. These sources also give us information about **identity** – who we are, and what being a man or woman means – because we learn about ourselves from the society around us.

The process of socialisation lasts our whole lifetime. We start to learn about the world from the moment we are born and it never stops – which is one of the reasons we can change our views, and why both society and language change. Learning about gender starts at a very early age. From birth onwards we are given certain types of toys, dressed in certain types of clothes, talked about and to in a certain way and told what behaviours are acceptable or not. As children we are bombarded with images which portray expectations about our future roles and preferences, with the sexes represented in very different ways. In other words, we quickly learn 'what we are for'. It is easy to think that the portrayal of girls and boys in traditional sex roles is no longer an acceptable or frequent occurrence. Unfortunately, this is far from true.

Activity

Look at the images from the toy sections of some popular Christmas catalogues from 1997 (pp. 36–37).

◎   What sex roles are being portrayed?
◎   Look at the names and nature of the products: what are the connotations?
◎   What skills would be learned by the children who played with these toys?

Commentary

You will notice that the girls are ironing, hoovering and caring for babies, while the boys are creating structures, playing with footballs and being super-heroes. The girls' toys are preparing them for domestic roles, while the boys are learning design and construction skills, as well as the notion that they could be powerful – sporting heroes, protective savers-of-the-world. The girls' world is an interior one, the boys are connected with outdoor activity.

    The family scene around the computer also gives us ideas about the roles expected: mum is glad everyone is happy so that she gets domestic harmony; dad wants to use the computer to explore; the boy already has games and this suggests that the computer is a central feature of his life of fun and games; the girl has used one at school – educational purposes only.

Text: Toy collage

Colour-coding is an important symbol of gender. In the original cata-logues, gender-stereotyped colours were used. There was lots of pink on the girls' pages and many of the products were pink or other 'feminine'

Text: Toy catalogue

colours such as primrose yellow or mauve, while boys' toys were often in darker, stronger colours such as dark blue or dark green, or else they had colour-coding with a specific reference, such as army combat colours.

Early learning about sex differences provides a strong grounding for beliefs about which social roles are 'natural' to men and women. However, the gendered portrayal of the sexes does not stop at childhood. Gender roles and preferences are reinforced by language and images throughout our lives: this means they are persistently confirmed, maintained and strengthened. The strength of this learning is reflected in the extent to which masculine or feminine behaviours and preferences have become a completely 'natural' part of our identity by the time we reach adulthood, and continue to be seen as such: it's 'only natural' that Jane should like babies, it's 'only natural' that Jim should like football; Jane is 'naturally' better than Jim at ironing, Jim is 'naturally' better than Jane at building cupboards. And 'it's only natural' that they should get together, of course.

Nowhere can we see the idea of 'natural' male and female preferences and behaviours better than in the way consumer products are marketed. Many products are targeted at male or female consumers with the idea that the product is 'naturally' the province of one sex or the other. The language used about these products and the names given all serve to reinforce their femininity or masculinity. A prime example of this is cosmetics, which have been strongly associated with women and femininity for a long time. 'Real men' do not wear make up – unless they're in army camouflage, drag or the Australian cricket team. So the language of cosmetic products such as lipstick, hairdye and nail varnish aimed at women often suggests a very traditional femininity, with ideas of delicacy and subtlety ('hint of a tint'), virginity and innocence ('peach blush') or the settings of popular romance novels, with their dreamy sunsets and pale heroines ('desert haze', 'white rose').

While face make up is still exclusively targeted at women consumers, other cosmetic products (such as deodorants, fragrances, soaps, bath/shower gels) often have a male range as well as a female one (as in the catalogue material in Unit one). In these cases, it is interesting to see how the male product differs from the female one in how it is named and described. Sometimes, what is effectively exactly the same product is described very differently, to construct a distinctively different picture of the **narratee** (the person supposedly addressed by the text). For example, one company markets a face cleanser for men called 'scruffing solution', presumably hoping to capture the idea of vigorous activity along with a devil-may-care attitude in the word 'scruffing', and the idea of problem-solving in the word 'solution', as well as creating a scientific-sounding name overall. Added together, we have an active, carefree/ rebellious, problem-solving, science-oriented narratee: not a bad profile for a 'real man' to aspire to.

Consider the language used in the promotional material for Aramis Lab Series For Men.

- What are the connotations of the names and descriptions?
- What ideas about the male consumer are being suggested here?
- How does the language used here differ from that of cosmetic products aimed at women?

Text: Aramis

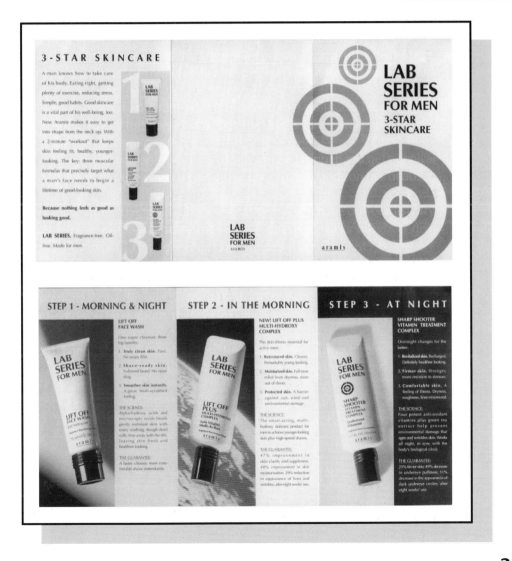

Fictional worlds

If the world is a gendered place in reality then this is likely to be reflected in fictive writing which is aiming for social realism. Such fiction, then, can be a good place to explore the ways in which language is gendered and to appreciate our ingrained beliefs about men and women. An added consideration is the power and status we ascribe to fiction: far from being a leisure pursuit that represents a minority interest, reading (or listening to and/or watching) stories represents a very common experience for all of us, and one that we appear to believe is very influential. If we didn't believe in the power of stories, then why have regulated and prescribed reading lists in school, why have endless debates on whether watching violent films is harmful, and why burn books and issue death-threats to writers because of what they have put in a work of fiction?

The act of reading itself appears to be quite a gendered activity, with men and women habitually reading different kinds of books, women favouring romance and modern novels, while men favour war, adventure and science fiction books, with the crime/thriller genre equally chosen by both sexes (Policy Studies Institute, 1989). But, as well as men and women having different domains in terms of genre, fiction books themselves regularly present men and women as distinctively different in behaviour and psychological traits.

Crossing the line between what we see as male and female domains in everyday life can startle us because it disrupts our habitual collocations: a woman in a jock-strap, or a man in a flowery dress throw, our expectations back into our faces, causing surprise, even shock. The fact that we notice a person because they are the 'wrong' sex can be seen as evidence of the gendered nature of the activity, behaviour, or role.

Activity

Switching pronouns in a text is a disruptive strategy which can demonstrate the power of beliefs about gender roles and characteristics associated with masculinity and femininity. In the two extracts below, all the pronouns have been switched, so that previously male characters are now referred to as 'she' and previously female characters are now 'he'.

◎ How have these changes altered the way the characters are presented?
◎ What do the changes tell you about the way the texts were previously gendered?

'You know what I'm talking about.' She was oddly elated, her eyes flashing down at him, her mouth curling at the edges with satisfaction.

Nervously he shook his head, the swing of his blonde hair against his cheek catching her eye. She shifted her hand to it, thrusting her fingers among the strands, winnowing them slowly and watching the way they drifted against her flesh.

'Don't lie to me, even if you've been lying to yourself.' Urgency deepened her voice and he felt a surge of panic begin inside him. 'Ever since I saw you at that window . . .'

'No!' he broke out, turning stumblingly away.

She pulled him back towards her, slamming him against her so abruptly that he fell, his face in her throat, his nostrils filling with the scent of her brown skin. Her hand gripped his back in a convulsive movement, the muscular tension of her body pressing against him.

'You looked fantastic. You're not ashamed of that are you? My God, you left me breathless!'

'Don't talk about it!' he begged.

'Why not, in God's name? For a second I thought you were a marble statue. It was the effect of the moonlight; you looked cool and remote and unreal. Then you moved and I felt as though someone had punched me in the stomach. You really knocked me out.'

He tried to pull away, trembling. 'Can't you see how embarrassing it is? I don't want to talk about it.'

'You're scared,' she whispered, her voice unsteady. 'Don't be. It's what you were born for, this feeling . . .'

'I just feel embarrassed,' he said angrily, struggling.

The elated excitement went out of her face and it darkened into impatience, her brows jerking together, her eyes staring at him with a glittering demand in them.

'That's not true. You just won't admit how you feel. Are you afraid of love?'

He threw caution to the wind, his temper hardening in his voice. 'You're not talking about love, you're talking about sex.'

'They're the same thing.'

(*Seduction,* Charlotte Lamb, p. 64-65)

Text: Extract 2

She couldn't wait to see him. But the moment he opened the door, looked at her and said, 'oh,' she felt her high begin to nose over.

All right, he was surprised, no question about it. She said, 'You're expecting someone.'

He said, 'No . . .' not sounding too sure. He said, 'Well, yes and no, but come on in.'

At this point there was still hope. He looked great.

'It's okay?'

'Yeah, really.'

But then closing the door he said, 'You want your gun, don't you?' and the good feeling sunk all the way to hit bottom as he went to the bedroom in his loose T-shirt and tight jeans saying, 'Let me get it.'

Like going to get change for the paper boy.

No apology or acting sheepish about it, wanting to explain. No - you want your gun? And goes to get it. She had come here prepared to treat it lightly. 'You get a chance to use that gun you stole on anybody?' Like that, with a straight face. Well, no fun and games now. It pissed her off, this act he put on, so fucking casual about it. Ask him how he'd like to go back to the Stockade, since Ordell hadn't paid the bond premium. See how casual he was then.

He came out of the bedroom with her gun in his hand and kind of a sad smile, saying, 'I'm sorry,' and she felt her mood begin to swing up again, hope stirring in her. 'I was afraid if I asked to borrow it you'd say no, and you'd have every right to. Would you like some coffee?'

Just like that, back in the game.

She said, 'I wouldn't mind,' following him to the kitchen. 'You get to use it?'

He gave her the smile again. 'I felt a lot safer having it. I hope you don't take milk. It turned sour while I was in jail.'

'No, black's fine.'

She watched him lay the Airweight on the kitchen table, bare except for an ashtray, and go to the range. He looked even slimmer in the jeans than he did last night. Not slim exactly, just right.

(*Rum Punch,* Elmore Leonard, p. 143-44)

Fictionalising ourselves

It's easy to look at published works of fiction, and decide that genderised descriptions of men and women are what other people do – but not us. The introduction to this unit suggested that we all 'do' gender on a daily basis, and this means all of us, not just people who create those texts that society considers important or powerful. The final activity in this unit will focus on some texts that anybody can write, and will explore the extent to which gender affects the way we fictionalise ourselves.

Activity

Write a personal ad for yourself, to be printed in a specified news-paper or magazine of your choice. Just write the first part – the self-description – and try to use fewer than 30 words. Use whatever abbreviations you know and consider appropriate. Do not identify your-self as male or female by either giving a name or any other reference to your sex.

If you are working in a group situation, mix up all the ads when everyone is finished, so that all the authors are anonymous. Then cat-egorise them according to the sex of the writer. Read them through and think about whether there are any patterns of information and self-description that recur within each sex group. If you can detect patterns of usage, consider why these might have occurred: why might men or women describe themselves in particular ways?

Now read the personal ads overleaf, which were taken from a local 'freesheet' newspaper. To what extent can you see any patterns here that suggest the writers are 'gendering' themselves? Also consider the descriptions of their desired partners: do these descriptions fall into any pattern?

One researcher (Shalom, 1997) has suggested that personal ads pages are a kind of supermarket where people are trading what they have for something they want. So what do the people below see as their saleable attributes?

43

Women seeking men

Female, 20, good body work, excellent suspension, goes when revved up, seeks male 24–30 to tinker with old banger.

Female, 28, large and lovely and lively, needs some TLC. I have been hurt in the past just need a friend to talk to, go out with, go for meals, dancing.

Red hair, blue eyes, slim. Interested? Then pick up the phone. I've got a GSOH and lots to say, 23-year-old lass looking for male 20-28 for friendship and who knows.

Two mad ladies looking for two men behaving badly.

Men seeking women

Male, 18, seeking blonde female for LTR. Must like pubs and nights in.

Wealthy amusing but busy company director, 40, seeks loving female for socialising.

Martin, single, 33, 6ft, OHOC, short hair, blue eyes, well built, looking for slim-medium female, honest, reliable and caring 24-33 for friendship maybe more. Single parents welcome.

Male, early forties, 5ft 7", OHOC but no woman. Can you help?

Summary

This unit has had as its focus the qualities and attributes that women and men are expected to have, and the way in which we circulate these expectations via language and images in many different contexts.

Extension

1   Make a collection of terms that you think tend to be used more of one sex than another. If possible, collect terms in context – that is, in use in texts such as newspapers, magazines, adverts, novels, radio and TV programmes, casual conversation, oral stories and jokes. For spoken texts, write down a record of the term within the utterance

where it occurred. Note who was speaking and the context of the conversation and, in the case of a broadcast text, details of the programme's content, channel, timing. Also collect terms that you think can be used of either sex, but which tend to mean something different when used of one sex or the other.

When you have collected more than a dozen terms, try them out on some informants, by repeating the activity you did on pages 30–1 of this unit.

2   Collect some examples of how men and women are referred to in the press or on TV or radio news broadcasts, during one day's news coverage. Choose for your focus two contrasting papers or channels in terms of their ideology/political persuasion.

3   Analyse some toy and clothes catalogues for children. What colours are being used and what types of clothing and activities are represented? Look carefully at the verbal language, including brand names, descriptions, slogans, logos. Focus on one particular type of toy – for example, bicycles – and, looking at the pages where bikes are displayed, see if you can spot which bikes are for girls and which for boys.

4   Collect some brand names and descriptions of cosmetic products aimed at adult men and women. Do they differ? If so, how? What constructions are being offered of the target audience in each case?

5   Focus on a particular genre of literary or film fiction and analyse the ways in which male and female characters are portrayed. You can learn a lot about the approach of a book or film just from its title and 'blurb' alone. If you list as many titles as you can find for a particular genre – for example, horror novels or films – you will soon get a sense of the concerns and outlook promoted by that genre. Film posters and trailers are especially revealing.

6   Look out particularly for texts that play around with the idea of gender, or that overturn traditional ideas. For example, there are now many women writers of detective fiction who have a female 'sleuth'. You could compare some of these figures with their conventional male counterparts. You could also investigate texts that deliberately shift perspectives, such as Virginia Woolf's *Orlando* (1928), which has a narrator who changes sex. Sometimes, writers have narrators who are a different sex from them – for example, Martin Amis has a female detective narrator (called 'Mike Hoolihan') in *Night Train* (1997), and Peter Hoeg does the same in *Miss Smilla's Feeling for Snow* (1995). Are these convincing? Do you think it is possible for people of one sex to write as another?

7   Collect some personal ads and analyse the effect of gender on the way information is selected and presented. These texts are inter-esting interfaces of many different social factors, so this activity is a chance to explore the way gender relates to other dimensions, such as sexuality (straight compared with gay and bisexual columns or publications), social class (newspapers with different social class readership), age (teenage magazines compared with those aimed at an older audience) and culture (texts written in English compared with those translated from another language).

8   Try to write a description of a person which does not use gendered language or subscribe to traditional sex roles. Extend this to include some action.

Unit three

All in the mind?

In this unit the relationship between thought and language, introduced in Unit one, is considered in more depth, in order to explore the thinking and associated language features involved in **stereotyping** and **marking**.

We can all think about something, but *how* we think and reason is more mysterious. The way our mind works is strongly related to our language and our culture, because it is through these that we perceive and understand the 'real world'. To appreciate this relationship it is necessary to consider some ideas about how the brain functions in relation to the world and language, and how language influences the way our brains organise information.

You will already have noticed that the two terms 'brain' and 'mind' have been used interchangeably above. In fact, these two terms have often been used historically to mean different things, and there are still many debates on how they differ. For example, 'brain' has often been used to denote biological and functional activities (like movement, speech production and memory), while 'mind' has often included more individual, creative and imaginative aspects of mental activity (like dreaming and thinking). There isn't space to enter this debate here, but it's important to mention that you will come across these terms in some academic traditions (such as that of psychology) as representing different things. However, in this book, we will be using the terms interchangeably.

The language of the mind

Thinking, memory, reasoning, perception, and other psychological processes that occur in the brain are referred to as aspects of **cognition**. Cognitive processes are involved in every aspect of how we interact with the world – how and what we perceive, understand, decide, and how we behave.

As far as we know, cognitive structures and processes do not *physically* exist, unlike biological or physiological structures and processes. There are parts of the brain that we know are associated with certain types of cognitive activity, like speech or sight, but how these actually function remains unclear. For example, when we 'see' and 'hear', we do something fairly amazing with the signals we receive from the world. Very simply, seeing involves signals in the form of light hitting parts of the eye, which causes cells in the eye to react (or **fire**) in a way that sets a chain of cell reaction up the optic nerve and into the brain. In the brain, our cognitive processes transform the firing of cells (**neurones**) into recognisable visual information – shapes, depth, size, colour, people, objects, movement, etc. This transformation into 'real' information occurs in a miniscule amount of time. Imagine if cognitive processes took so long that there was a perceivable delay between 'seeing' something and 'knowing' that you could see it. Trying to touch an object in front of us would be difficult, especially if it was moving, walking would be hazardous and driving would be lethal.

As we can't physically 'get to' our cognitive processes, we only have theories about how they work, based upon the evidence provided by data – our everyday experiences of thinking, talking, dreaming and imagining – as well as scientific studies. There are specific areas of the brain which we know are involved in understanding and producing language, but we still don't know *how* language is understood or stored. In fact, we know very little about the brain as a whole, especially compared to the knowledge we have of other processes and structures, such as the heart and lungs and how oxygen and carbon dioxide are exchanged in the bloodstream.

Activity

The aim of this activity is to get you to think about how we think about thinking! The particular focus is to explore the idea that the ways we think, or conceptualise, are based upon the language that we have and the culture that we are in.

Look at the terms below, which are all ways that we talk about our brains. All the terms are metaphors, which are ways of talking about something in terms of something else. The first group of terms are older than the second.

◎   What are the two sets of metaphors based on?
◎   Why do you think we use metaphorical language to talk about our brains?
◎   Does it make any difference which metaphors we use to describe ourselves? Should we really be using metaphors at all?

Group 1

I can't get my brain into gear
I'm only firing on two cylinders
I'm a bit rusty
I need to get the cogs turning

Group 2

my memory is full
let me process the information
I'm in active mode today
I need to switch off for a minute

Commentary

Both sets of metaphors are based upon the idea of the brain as a machine, but the first group are based on 'old' technology and the second group on 'new' technology such as computers. Neither group of terms describes anything real in the sense of describing what our brains are really doing: metaphors are forms of figurative language that we often use when we want to turn something abstract into something concrete and understandable. For example, we often talk about our emotions, which are also abstract entities, in metaphorical terms such as 'I really boiled over', 'I had steam coming out of my ears', or 'I exploded', when we talk about anger. Some linguists, for example, Lakoff (1987), maintain that most of our everyday language is in fact metaphorical.

Although these phrases seem 'real' to us, they are just one way of representing the world to ourselves, and they are culture-specific. It is no accident that we now talk about our brains as if they were computers, since this new technology is so pervasive, and especially since scientists themselves have been using the computer as a model for the brain for some time. Scientific discourses are no more 'real' than any others, despite their persuasive power in society.

But imagine that our society was all focused on horticulture – we might talk about our brains in the following ways:

I can't think, I need fertilising
I have ideas budding
my brain needs pruning
I need repotting

If we described ourselves as plants instead of machines, we might see ourselves quite differently. For example, we might expect our brains to be quite dormant for part of the year, and to become more active in the 'growing season'.

The main points to carry forward from this exercise are that:

◎ abstract ideas and processes – such as thinking – are often described metaphorically, because they are hard to 'get at';
◎ if we look at the language used to describe something, we can gain an understanding of the way that thing is being conceptualised by the members of that culture;
◎ concepts are not 'real' (although they seem it), but are constructed using social experience;
◎ our concepts produce consequences for us.

Cognition and language

Language and linguistic knowledge are cognitive components, just like memory and imagination. However, language actually plays a very important and fundamental role in cognition because language influences the way in which we organise our cognitive system - this means that language influences the way the brain organises thought and knowledge.

Like all large masses of knowledge (like libraries, computers, etc.) the brain has a system of organisation to enable the location, retrieval and use of the information it contains. The basis of the brain's cognitive system is categories and, since categories are labelled linguistically, this means language influences our thinking and reasoning via the process of categorisation.

Why do we categorise?

The world is a highly complex place. So many things happen in it at one time that it is impossible to comprehend everything. In cognitive terms this means that we cannot process *all* the information or data that we are receiving from our senses at the same time - even the data just from our eyes *or* ears is too much. To enable us to function and understand what is happening in the world, we need to both simplify and become selective about what information gets processed and how far it gets processed. For example, what gets processed to the extent that we notice it, pay attention to it and consciously think about it.

Categorising allows us to generate 'everyday' thinking which is automatic, quick and effortless, without which interacting with the world would become a long and laborious process. Categories exist for everything - people, objects, events, emotions, language components, etc. When we come across something unknown we make an effort to find out information that enables us to categorise it so we can understand what it is.

Activity

Imagine a situation where you have come across an object that you cannot recognise – you have no idea what it is or what it does. What questions might you ask about it? Can you think of a question you might ask that does not seek to categorise the object?

Now think about how you might explain an unknown object or phenomenon to another person – like snow or a car or a dress. Can you do it without referring to the categories it belongs to?

Commentary

The process of categorisation involves the grouping together of 'things' that are related. This means we must have some basis for believing these things to be related – a concept or **cognitive model** which puts these things together in a group. In this way, a linguistic category also embodies a cognitive model. So, with reference to the previous items, linguistic categories of types of weather conditions, types of vehicle and types of clothing all embody cognitive models.

51

Keeping it simple

'Everyday' thinking and language use simplified category models – a few 'rules of thumb' to serve as a cognitive 'short cut'. Unfortunately, simplifying also means having to lose information and make general assumptions, which means the loss of individual detail. We simplify using social knowledge. This means that cultural values and beliefs provide the basis for the simplifications and general rules embodied in cognitive models, even if we 'know' that things are not really that simple. For example, traditional 'stick figures' representing men and women use a skirt and long hair to denote female. We know that the reality of women with long hair and skirts is no longer a true reflection of society – but we understand the concepts being represented and who the symbols represent. It is such shared cognitive models which allow us to use non-word symbols as representations of categories.

Activity

The symbols opposite have all been used to represent men and women, many of them on toilet doors. Look at the symbols, decide which represents the man or the woman, and then discuss what cognitive models or cultural concepts they embody (that is, what shared social knowledge is encoded).

Commentary

You might have realised that some of the symbols only work when used with another matched symbol or label, like the glasses. One of the pairs of symbols is from another country and you may have found it harder to decide which is male or female, and why. The circle and triangle are the Polish symbols for women and men, respectively. It is unclear how Polish people 'rationalise' these symbols: one piece of anecdotal evidence given to us by a group of Polish teachers was that 'men have broad shoulders and women are rounded'.

There are also verbal labels which only work properly in context, or which play writing off against speech. For example, the following denoting of men's and women's toilets has been observed in seaside restaurants with nautical themes: inboard and outboard motors; buoys and gulls. There are many types of gender coding, colour being one common and powerful form.

Text: Symbols

Constructing categories

Categories, especially social categories, actually only exist because they are viewed as culturally significant. A category can also only exist in contrast with something else, that is they would not exist if there was no alternative. For example, if there was only one sex then there would be no sex category. Equally, if race was not significant politically then the use of the categories of 'black' and 'white' would not be used to refer to or describe people. This may sound a bit odd, that such apparently obvious perceptual or biological distinctions as male or female, black or white, might not be made. But the categories which are used in a society are a reflection of what the society *believes* to be important about people; beliefs which are based upon its political and social order - its **ideology**.

Support for the idea that categories reflect culture rather than 'physical reality' has been provided by cross-cultural studies. Evidence shows that if a category is not socially important then it is not used to describe or differentiate people. This also means that any category could become important depending upon the beliefs a society develops. For example, if 'handedness' was a significant social category, this would be used to distinguish people. In fact in the past this was an important category, left-handedness was viewed as evil and a 'sign of the devil', and schoolchildren often had their left hand tied behind their back so they would have to write with their right hand.

Even when a category, like gender, is shared by most cultures it does not mean that there are shared attitudes towards that category. This means that the cognitive model embodied in a shared category can vary between cultures. The idea that women are not suitable to do 'heavy work' is only relevant in cultures where women are seen as physically weaker. In some cultures women do the heavy work that is often considered unsuitable in places like Britain. However, this does not mean that these cultures necessarily view men and women as equal. In fact it may be quite the opposite, with women doing heavy, unskilled work because they are seen as socially inferior.

Such evidence suggests that the way we think is socially constructed, that is based upon social experience and power relations rather than a literal representation of the physical world and its 'natural order'. This extends to many concepts we have about the world and the way we live within it. For example, the idea that 'time is money' is a metaphor based upon Western concepts of work, financial profit and financial reward. Even apparently basic concepts, like time and the way it moves, vary across societies and cultures. The notion that time moves forward - that there is a past, present and future - or that it is divided into hours, minutes and seconds is not shared by all cultures.

The power of cognitive models

Even though cognitive models are very simplified constructions of the world, they contain a tremendous amount of information and have a powerful impact on the way we think, yet most of the time we are unaware of them: how often do you actually consider what 'time' is, how it moves and what we mean when we say things like 'I haven't got time', 'time flies' or that we've 'run out of time'?

The power of cognitive models comes from the fact that we take them for granted. We learn them through socialisation and language acquisition so that social knowledge is mainly integrated into the ways we think without us being aware. For example, in Britain we don't tend to think of 'rat', 'horse', or 'insect' as members of the food category, but there are parts of the world where these items are considered delicacies. In the same way, some cultures regard the eating of pork as disgusting, the eating of beef as sacrilegious, or the idea of consuming meat at all as abhorrent. Food is an area where cultural norms and social values can strongly influence what we think of as fitting the category, and where cognitive models vary enormously across cultures. Models also vary through time. For example, a great delicacy in Tudor Britain was swan; nowadays, we are more likely to feed them bread than stuff them with it for the oven.

It is the embodiment of cultural concepts in the cognitive model, and hence language, which underlies the reason why language is not neutral – because *attitudes and beliefs are part of the cognitive model*. The cognitive model embodied in a category is usually obvious to the members of the society or culture, so obvious it does not even need to be consciously thought about. It is only when a cognitive model does not fit with the situation that we tend to consciously pay attention and 'think about it'; that is when the object, event or situation is not typical. This is a bit like seeing a three-legged dog, we tend to notice it because in our cognitive model dogs have four legs. A 'typical' dog is the cognitive model.

Typicality

Although categories appear to be quite simple things, the way they work is actually quite complex. For a start, categories are not clear-cut and exclusive, instead they often share members and have sub-categories. There are also category members (**hyponyms**) which we think of as more typical or more central than other members. The central members are those which fit the cognitive model or category best, and these are the basis for our idea of 'the **norm**'. For example, when the category 'bird' is mentioned most people think of a robin or a sparrow - rather than a penguin or a chicken - because robins and sparrows fit our norm model of a bird more precisely. These members are said to have central status in the category.

Activity

To explore the nature of categories and their group members, look at the data below.

For each group, try to arrive at a rank order for which of the group members is the best example of that category, then at the bottom of the list put the group member who least fits into that category.

When you have finished, try to explain your rationale for the rank order you have established for each group.

Pets	Birds	Parts of the body	Furniture	Vehicles	Advert
dog	ostrich	hair	chair	car	branded carrier bag
spider	finch	head	stool	bicycle	TV commercial
cat	seagull	leg	table	skateboard	film trailer
snake	turkey	fingers	lamp	truck	university prospectus

Commentary

There is no right or wrong answer to this activity. The point is to think about how your cognitive models affected the way in which you assessed the group members. For example, if your concept of 'birdiness' excludes edibility, then you will have put the turkey at the bottom (but note that finches are also eaten in some cultures, as is ostrich); if 'birdiness' for you is strongly about flight and small size, then ostrich will be low on the list and finch high.

Some other rank orders might relate to ideas about dependency and secondary status: for example, hair is attached to the head, so 'hair' might seem dependent or secondary to the more important group member, 'head'. In the same way, a lamp sits on a table and a stool could be seen as a chair with the back missing, so lamp and stool could be seen as secondary in these cases. It all depends on how you conceptualise the items.

56

Central status is not necessarily about items that are typical because they are common in our own experience; it is more about the fact that they distill a number of qualities that we see as essential to the definition, and, for this reason, are at the basis of frequent cultural representations. For example, you may never have seen a finch in reality, but the idea of a small, fluttery, pretty creature that sings attractively may fit your concept of 'birdiness' better than the lumbering, noisy, rather unappealing turkey or ostrich. And for this very reason, people who want to suggest 'birdiness' in visual texts may choose that particular bird a lot, so that we think it is common and typical. You can see this process operating with the robin, who turns up unfailingly on British Christmas cards as a stocky, cheeky little creature with a red breast.

The cognitive models which represent these 'typical' or 'central' members are called **prototypes**, and it is usually prototypical models that come to mind when a category is called up. This means that prototypes can often represent the whole category in our thinking.

From prototypical to stereotypical

As well as categorising objects, we also categorise people into groups where some group members are seen as more typical or representative than others, even though in reality they may be in the minority. When we construct a simplified and limited model from the characteristics of a few group members and apply these to the whole group, what we are doing is stereotyping. Stereotypes are often exaggerated, composite pictures that share many of the qualities of caricature. Stereotyping is very much about the process of applying a simplified model to a real, complex individual, often to negative and derogatory effect. So, forms of 'cognitive shorthand' or 'rules of thumb' which are useful to us in other ways in order to simplify the world become applied as sets of very restricting generalisations which suppress individual complexity. Stereotypes gain power and credibility through wide use in everyday talk and texts as a result of the fact that they are 'well-understood or easy-to-perceive' (Lakoff, 1987: 77), rather than because they are true. Obviously, this is not just a psychological process that operates in a vacuum: our stereotypes are very bound up with the social and political structures of our culture. This can be seen in the Jak cartoon, which relies for its effect on a number of social stereotypes.

Text: Jak cartoon I

"It's about your sexist attitude, Valerie. Now you've upset the scaffolders!"

31 December 1991

Building-site workers were threatened with the sack if they indulged in sexist pastimes, like wolf-whistling at passing women and sticking up posters of nude women.

Mark my words

The whole process of categorising, with its reliance on typicality, is very strongly connected with the way linguistic items are marked in various ways in order to indicate what is 'normal' and what is **deviant.**

The first point to make is that marking can be covert as well as overt: that is, linguistic meanings can derive as much from their structural relationships as from the specific markings that occur on the words themselves. The activities that follow will illustrate these different aspects.

Activity

There are many pairs of terms in English that act as **antonyms**, where one term is unmarked and the other marked. The unmarked term is the term that would be used in straightforward questions and statements, while the marked term reflects an unusual or particular meaning. So, for example, in the pair of terms to describe age – 'old' and 'young', the unmarked term is 'old' in the following:

How old are you?

If you used the term 'young' in the same structure, the implied meaning would be very different – not a straightforward question about age, but a question where the youth of the interloctor has already been established:

How young are you?

Now read through the antonyms in the sentences below. Decide which is the unmarked and which the marked term in each case. Also decide what the marked term might be implying, by describing a context where the marked example might occur:

How tall are you?
How short are you?

How heavy is that parcel?
How light is that parcel?

How fast does this car go?
How slow does this car go?

How big is the pay rise going to be?
How small is the pay rise going to be?

Can you think of any further pairs of words that act in the same way?

Activity

This activity will familiarise you with more overt linguistic marking, in the form of modification. Think about the ordinary term 'mother'. Write down what you see as its denotation and connotations. When you have done this, read through the terms overleaf and decide, for each one, how the addition of a descriptive item alters the image of the mother being represented:

working mother   surrogate mother   stepmother
foster mother godmother biological mother adoptive mother single mother
housemother (a woman with a pastoral role in a school - usually a public school)

Commentary

The markings in each of the phrases above are used to tell us that the label departs from some unstated 'norm' or typical situation. Often it is very useful to examine marked items as a way to get back to what is at the basis of the unmarked term.

For example, the phrase 'working mother' suggests that the norm for 'mother' is someone who stays at home to look after the children and does not have paid employment. (One question often asked wryly about the literal meaning of the phrase 'working mother' is: is there any other kind?) The phrase 'single mother' tells us that the 'ideal' is marriage or partnership.

Other phrases above appear to deviate from an idea of 'naturalness' that is to do with a combination of two factors: being a biological parent, and nurturing and caring for a child. In each case above, one of these two factors is missing. So a godmother, stepmother, foster mother, housemother and adoptive mother may all look after a child's welfare, but they are not the child's biological parent. A surrogate mother and biological mother have biological connections, but the implications are that this is the point where it ends.

So the unmarked term 'mother' can be seen as representing a norm of: staying at home, not being in paid employment, being in a relationship, being the biological parent and nurturing and caring for the child. You could therefore say that 'mother' is our unmarked term which represents a kind of default model – that is, the meaning we return to if no other marking is present.

Activity

What do the following marked expressions on the right tell us about the meaning of the unmarked term on the left? In turn, what does the existence of all these pairs of terms tell us about the relationship between gender and the social and political structures of our society?

nurse	male nurse
prostitute	male prostitute
doctor	woman doctor
priest	woman priest
secretary	male secretary
model	male model
boy	toy boy
girl	career girl

There are other forms of marking that are more clearly part of the **morphological** system of English: for example, **suffixes** such as 'ess' and 'ette'. We have pairs of terms where the unmarked form is male, and the marked form female. Not only does this suggest that the male figure is the 'norm' and the female one 'deviant', but the female form clearly has derived status and, in the case of 'ette', implies diminution or imitation (cigarette is a small cigar, suedette is 'false' suede). Read through the pairs below, and say whether you think the words in each pairing have equal value in terms of the social status of their referents.

manager	manageress
usher	usherette
actor	actress
god	goddess
lad	ladette
waiter	waitress
mayor	mayoress
master	mistress

Cognition and reference

This final section will look at the idea of **generic** and **sex-specific reference** in terms of our thinking and language use. Later in the section we will be concentrating on pronouns, but to start with we will look at the distribution of the terms 'man/boy' and 'woman/girl' in everyday phrases and sayings in English. A common theme for the whole section is how we refer to people when we don't want to name them specifically, but just suggest a hypothetical male or female figure.

Text: Lost consonants

Graham Rawle's **LOST CONSONANTS**

(33) One of man's earliest inventions was the heel

Activity

Fill in the missing word or word-parts in the phrases below and think about what they mean and why they are so familiar to us. Can you think of any other phrases or idioms that reflect our societal concepts of gendered work, domestic roles and appropriate social behaviour?

Because these sayings are so familiar, it might help you to turn them round when you have filled them in, by making them apply to the opposite sex, and think about the effect of the changes you have made. Many of the phrases below are using man/boy or woman in a sex-specific sense: in other words, the intended meaning is 'male people' or 'female people'. But in some cases, it could be argued that 'man' is being used generically – that is, to suggest 'people in general'. What do you think?

A __ place is in the home   That's no job for a __
It's a __ world   Best __ for the job
May the best __ win   One of the __
Chair__ of the Board   Take it like a __
__ will be __   The old __ network

Activity

Now read through the phrases below, and think about the following questions:

◎   what pictures are created in your mind as you process the meaning of each example? For example, do you 'see' men, women, or both sexes?;

◎   which of the phrases are most strongly sex-specific? Are there any that work generically?

Neanderthal man
Man breastfeeds his young
Man and machine in perfect harmony
Of mice and men
Man needs food, water and shelter to survive
A small step for a man, a giant leap for mankind
If man was meant to fly he'd have been given wings
An Englishman's home is his castle
A gentleman's agreement
Man overboard
A man-made environment
A man's best friend is his dog
The man in the street
The average working man

Gender, generics and grammatical rules

Sometimes when writers use the term 'gender' in talking about grammar, they are referring to the way some languages give nouns a specific gender, which is marked structurally. For example, in German, the word for 'lamp' - *die Lampe* - is female, while the word for 'table' - *der Tisch* - is male. These categories bear no relation to the idea of gender as we are using the term here. However, our idea of gender and the subject of grammar are strongly connected in another way, and that is the ruling of early English grammarians that the noun 'man' and the pronoun 'he' should be used not only to refer to men but also for general reference, to refer to 'all persons'. Their justification for this rule was that it represented the 'natural order of things':

> Some will set the Carte before the horse, as thus. My mother and my father are both at home, even thoughe the good man of the house ware no breaches or that the graye Mare were the better Horse. And what thoughe it often so happeneth (God wotte the more pitte) yet in speaking at the leaste, let us kepe a natural order, and set the man before the woman for maners Sake.
>
> (Wilson, 1560: 189 cited in Bodine, 1975: 128)

This grammatical rule was the subject of parliamentary legislation in 1850, and has been handed down to us via rules of 'correct' usage in grammar books. One result of this is that we have had a long history of seeing certain usages as good or bad, right or wrong English simply in terms of grammar rules, rather than as good or bad language in terms of how people were represented or referred to in communication and thinking. Also, grammar rules are one thing, but real English is another. People have regularly used 'they' as a way of getting round the pronoun problem when speaking, even in formal contexts. For example, here is what you hear on the telephone if you dial 1471 to find out who has phoned you, and the caller has left no 'trace':

> You were called today at [time]. The caller withheld *their* number.

In terms of traditional grammar rules, the sentence above has been seen historically as incorrect because the plural 'they' is being coupled with the singular noun 'caller'. However, it has more often been written rather than spoken usage where contestations have arisen. And even now, with our modern acceptance of the need for change, supposedly sex-generic 'he'/'his' and 'man' are more likely to crop up in official written documents and institutional discourse than elsewhere. The problem is that such discourse very much has the stamp of authority and 'truth'.

Activity

Even though you might be a thoughtful user of 'generic' language, the next activity will help you to understand the work on cognition that follows; it will also help you to understand the perspective of Unit four.

The first extract below is from a Sunday colour supplement article about management team work; the second is from an 'English for Commerce' exam paper from 1986.

What might be the different effects (intended or otherwise) of the following changes to the texts?:

◎ making all the pronouns plural – i.e., 'they';
◎ using 'he or she' all the way through;
◎ reversing the pronoun usage, so that 'he' changes to 'she', and vice versa;
◎ using 'she' all the way through;
◎ other strategy – specify which.

If you are working in a group situation, you could each take one of the strategies above and rework the texts, then compare your results. There is no commentary on this activity because what follows is some explanatory information on generic forms and cognition.

Extract 1
Any attempt to list the qualities of a good manager demonstrates why he cannot exist: far too many of the qualities are mutually exclusive. He must be highly intelligent and he must not be too clever. He must be highly forceful and he must be sensitive to people's feelings. He must be dynamic and he must be patient. He must be a fluent communicator and a good listener.... And if you do find this jewel among managers, this paragon of mutually incompatible characteristics, what will you do when he steps under a bus, or goes to live abroad for the sake of his wife's health, or leaves to take up a better job with your principal competitor?

Extract 2
The telephonist is judged by the caller to be representative of the organisation by which she is employed, and if a telephone enquirer does not receive a clear and courteous greeting he immediately tends to form a bad impression of the organisation as a whole. Tact is necessary to avoid putting undesired calls through to high-level executives of the organisation. The private secretary is responsible for shielding her employer from unnecessary calls which will waste his time.

Generics and cognition

From a social psychological and cognitive perspective, the crux of the issue should not be about what is grammatically 'correct', particularly since grammatical rules are 'man-made'. Instead, the issue should be about who is represented in thought when these terms are actually used – that is, who is represented cognitively.

Studies have shown that generic usage does not readily invoke a generic meaning – that is, using 'he' or 'him' and 'man' or 'men' in neutral contexts results in most people thinking of a man (for example, Khosroshahi, 1989). 'They' has been found to more readily suggest a mixture of both men and women, although 'he/she' and 'humans' comes out best at ensuring people think about women as well. Even in cases where we 'know' that 'man' is meant generically, we still tend to think 'male'. This is because the unmarked form is male which means we immediately and automatically think male until we realise it's meant to be generic. Even then, a generic reading is a secondary reading, and this fact has important implications for us cognitively, not least because additional cognitive processing or effort is required for the generic usage to be perceived and then under-stood.

This secondary processing of the generic meaning may seem relatively trivial if we just take into account the miniscule amount of time it actually takes to perceive a generic meaning as opposed to a male-specific reading. However, cognitively and socially the impact of this first male reading has important implications – because it means we think male unless context or linguistic marking suggests otherwise. The prob-lem with context as an indication of generic intent is that too often the reading can be both specific and generic. This means that there are many instances where an intended generic reading will be missed as the male-specific reading makes sense (since this is processed first and the secondary reading will only occur if no sense can be made). For example, 'best man for the job', can easily be read as male-specific, so any intended generic reading can disappear. The force of male-specific reading is well illustrated in the slogan that was carried on a march in Paris by women wanting to remind people that half the population was female:

One in two men is a woman.

Many men thought this was a statement that was questioning their masculinity.

So why do male pronouns and other supposedly generic terms automatically invoke male cognitive models? As children, the first members of a category that we learn are usually the prototypes – the models which will dominate our thinking in unmarked contexts. In the case of male pronouns and other generic terms we learn their sex-specific meaning long before we learn their potentially generic meaning. This means that the male-specific meaning is the prototype.

Some researchers have claimed that the use of male terms in supposedly generic contexts functions to exclude women from language, rendering them 'cognitively invisible' (Ng, 1990) – that is, it excludes them from thought. But although they can 'disappear' in generic contexts, female figures clearly do feature in texts via specifically female reference such as the pronoun 'she'. For example, in both the texts you rewrote, female figures were mentioned. In both cases, though, the hypothetical women were pictured in dependent roles – secretary, wife. So the question of pronouns and other linguistic reference items is not just about generic or specific reference; it is also about the way we distribute such items throughout the texts we write and speak, for this gives us a sense of what male and female figures do in the world – to couch this in terms of the work you did in Unit two – a sense of 'what men and women are for'.

Summary

This unit has provided more information about the ways in which our language is far from neutral. Although the relationship is complex, you should now have some understanding of the way in which language embodies our cultural and social values and the way we invoke these automatically in our thinking. It should be clear that language is not a direct reflection of any natural order but a daily enactment of a social one. This means that when we speak, we don't just say words, we speak our culture. This idea will be taken up again in the next unit on 'political correctness'.

Extension

1   Investigate the way symbols work in computer contexts, for example:

◉   The symbols below are metaphors for a certain type of elec-
     tronic communication: do you know which it is, and how the
     symbols are metaphorical?

67

◎   What other metaphorical uses do we have in electronic communication, and why?

◎   Whose language and culture have formed the basis for computer communication? For example, we talk about 'surfing the net'; many of the technological developments in the computer world have come from the west coast of America. Do you think we might have had 'ski-ing the net', if computer industries had been developed in Scandinavia? Whose culture is represented by the symbols below?

2   Research to what extent people picture typical figures for certain occupations. You could do this by asking people to describe the ideal characteristics of the occupants of some chosen jobs, such as the following:

Police officer	Car mechanic	Lawyer	Chef
Soldier	Beautician	Journalist	Cook
Child minder	Gardener	Surgeon	Engineer
Farmer	Midwife	Priest	Computer programmer

Certain titles within some occupational settings are actually gendered terms, for example, the nursing rank of 'Sister'. What are male nurses who reach the position of Sister called? Are there other similarly gendered terms – what about the qualifications of 'Bachelor of Arts' and 'Master of Arts'?

You could give your research a good linguistic focus by looking at some job ads and seeing whether job titles appear to suggest a male or female figure as the ideal applicant. This would entail not just looking at obvious terms such as 'waitress/waiter', but also at whether gender is implied in the qualities being asked for – for example, 'bubbly, bright personality', 'stamina', etc.

3   Do a survey of young children's books like 'ABC' and early reading books to see what category members and cognitive models are portrayed. Pay particular attention to the types of people shown in different social roles, and how they are seen to speak to each other

4   Research how our common titles – Mr, Ms, Mrs, Miss – are marked and used: what are the origins of these terms? What information do they carry? What are current attitudes towards them and uses of them? Are there differences in spoken and written usage?

Political correctness

This unit aims to explore the complex issue called 'political correctness', so that you are better able to analyse what people mean when they use this phrase.

Brainstorm as many examples of political correctness in language use as you can. If possible, work with a partner or in a group situation, so that you can jog each other's memory about terms that you have heard. When you have finished, have your list beside you to refer to as you work through the material that follows.

Where did the term 'political correctness' come from?

According to Deborah Cameron (1995), the term 'political correctness' was originally used in a disapproving way by left-wing groups in the 1960s and 1970s to refer to their own group members who toed the party line very strictly and whose behaviour was therefore seen as 'ultra correct'. But, as Cameron points out, the phrase has undergone 'discursive drift', so that it no longer means one thing and one thing only. For example, the term has been used frequently, particularly since the 1980s, by right-wing commentators whose intention has been to criticise aspects of social reform.

What follows is an exploration of some of the recurrent themes underlying discussions of political correctness where *language* is at issue.

Language myths

One aspect of the debate to clear up straight away is that there have been many examples of so-called 'political correctness' in language use that are completely fictional: in other words, not all the examples of terms you are likely to have come up with have ever been used in real communication contexts. In many cases, terms have been invented in order to criticise those who wanted to make changes. Made-up terms have often involved very exaggerated uses. This is a familiar technique in satire: taking ideas to extremes can be an effective way to ridicule them. Here are some examples of *fictional cases*.

During the 1980s there were reports in the right-wing press that various 'loony left' London councils did the following:

◎ banned the word 'manhole' because it was sexist;
◎ banned the terms 'black coffee', 'blackboard' and 'black bin liners' because they were racist;
◎ banned the nursery rhyme 'baa baa black sheep' for the same reason (see the Jak cartoon).

Cameron points out that where serious journalists have tried to verify such allegations, they have discovered them to be unfounded. But, she claims, examples such as these take a hold to the extent that people don't question their authenticity. So, in effect, such stories and terms take on a life of their own as we pass them on to each other as anecdotes. This process is similar to the way we tell each other stories about supposedly real happenings, but where the events in question turn out to be what some commentators have called **urban myths** – fairy stories for a modern age. Here is one example. This story is often set on Dartmoor, but story-tellers vary on where the story is supposed to have occurred. For example, a German exchange student we taught insisted it happened in the Black Forest in Germany.

A man and woman are driving in a car that runs out of petrol. The road is dark and deserted, and the man takes a can and goes to get some petrol, telling his wife to lock the car doors and wait for him.

At the time of the story, there is a dangerous, mentally disturbed prisoner on the loose. After a long wait, the woman hears a strange thumping noise on the roof of the car. Then she sees a police car draw up and a loudhailer tells her to come out of the car, go towards the police car and not look back. She gets out and runs away from the car, but, as she does so, she can't help looking back. What she sees when she does so is a deranged man sitting on the roof of her car, playing ball with her husband's severed head.

Activity

Brainstorm any stories you have heard like the one above. Where did you hear the story, and how did the storyteller convince you it was true? Here are the 'abstracts' of some further stories you might have heard:

◎ the Chinese restaurant where the customer points to his poodle in order to get the dog a drink, but the dog is taken away and cooked for the customer's dinner;

◎ the young woman who goes to see a male stripper and gets genital crabs in her eye when a pair of his underpants lands on her head.

Now think about the 'politically correct' terms you have on your list. Try to remember where you heard the terms – did the speaker or writer give you any evidence? How do you know the terms really exist? Below are some more mythical examples. Did you have any of these on your list? What about the earlier terms that were supposed to have come from London councils: did any of these feature in your brainstorm and, if so, where did you hear about them originally?:

◎ having to substitute 'person' for 'man', as in, for example, 'person-chester' instead of 'Manchester', 'personfully' instead of 'manfully', etc.;

◎ phrases involving the word 'challenged' as in, for example, 'physically challenged' instead of 'disabled', 'vertically challenged' instead of 'short', etc.

Commentary: urban myths and language myths

You could say that what connects these two sorts of myths is the idea of fear. Urban myths are often about modern fears, such as that of psychopathic killers and sexually transmitted diseases. The myth about the Chinese restaurant rehearses the theme of xenophobia via the 'horrifying' nature of foreign eating customs. These modern urban tales are often likened to fairy tales because the latter are also about fears – of abandonment, of death, of the cruelty of the adult world, and so on.

But it is not enough to say that urban myths are about fears, for we need to ask whose fears they articulate. In the Chinese restaurant myth, it is the fear experienced by the Westerner that gets expressed. What about the male stripper story? You could see this as acting as a kind of warning to girls against sexual promiscuity, in the same way that the 'Little Red Riding Hood' story warns girls to stay on the straight and narrow.

In the same way, myths about politically correct language embody the fears that particular groups of people feel. They are often expressions of fear by the more powerful groups in society that the status quo might have to change, and not in their favour. So these language myths often derive from right-wing sources, and they satirise ideas about the claims of less powerful groups – women, black people, disabled people. In this case, then, political correctness is all about resisting or denying the claims of such groups to a share in power.

Linguistic neutrality?

The idea that links together all the work you have done so far in this book is that language is not 'neutral'. While it may reflect reality in the sense that it reflects how we have organised society, for the same reason, it does not reflect equality, because the different social groups that make up our culture have not been treated equally. So for many years, groups and individuals who have been working for equality have periodically focused on language in order to change attitudes and raise awareness of discrimination. It's important to stress that language reform has never been seen as an end in itself, but as part of a larger attempt to change the power relationships in society.

Reforming language

Calls for language reforms have been made by many different groups, not just by feminists. Since this is a book on language and gender, analysis of language as it relates to men and women is our central focus. But you will already have noticed that the issue of political correctness and language reform is one that cuts across the representation of a variety of groups.

Groups calling for language reforms in order to work towards more equal opportunities for the sexes have often differed in their strategies and in the degree of reform they have thought necessary. The material that follows aims to give you an understanding of the two main traditions within this area. Both of these traditions have produced examples of new language items that some commentators might label as 'politically correct'.

The liberal tradition

A very moderate, liberal approach can be seen in the work of Casey Miller and Kate Swift, who wrote *The Handbook of Non-Sexist Writing* (1981), a book which has served as a guide for serious journalists for many years. The rationale for this liberal tradition is that it is possible for language to be made more representative of different groups and, in order to bring about fairer representation, language practices need to be changed in various ways. This sometimes mean inventing new terms where old ones will not do.

Below are the main areas put forward as needing attention. In some cases, you will be referred back to Unit three, as some aspects mentioned below have already been covered there. See whether any of the suggestions below for new job titles occurred in your original brainstorm on 'political correctness'. The difference between these examples and the phrases previously called 'language myths' is that the job titles below were intended for real use and have in many cases been used in public and official contexts.

1   *The use of 'man' as a false generic* (see Unit three).
2   *The pronoun problem* (see Unit three).
3   *Discriminatory job titles.* Examples (with alternatives, taken from the United States Dept of Labor *Job Title Revisions*, 3rd edn., 1975). Note that the revisions were trying to combat ageism as well as sexism.

Original term	New term
airline steward, stewardess	flight attendant
foreman	supervisor
salesman	salesperson
seamstress	sewer
signalman	signaller
watchman	guard
draftsman	drafter
junior executive	executive trainee
camera man	camera operator
office girl, boy	office helper
repairman	repairer
fireman	firefighter
spokesman	spokesperson
policeman	police officer
chairman	chairperson, chair
housewife	house manager

4   *Generalisations.* This is where, although no specific sex-reference is present, writers have obviously got a specific group in mind, and are generalising from that group to everyone. Examples:

◎   'The average person finds it no problem at all to have three headcolds, one sunburn, an attack of athlete's foot, 20 headaches, three hangovers and five temper tantrums with

adolescent children, and still get in his 61 hours of shaving.'
- ◎ 'H.G. Wells has the ability to exert his magnetism on the small boy in all of us.'
- ◎ 'Sharing our railway compartment were two Norwegians and their wives.'

5   *Non-parallel treatment.* Miller and Swift divide this aspect into several areas, as below. Limitations of space prevent a long list of examples, but you should be familiar with these ideas as a result of the work you did on newspapers in Unit two:

- ◎ describing women by appearance, but men by achievement;
- ◎ describing women by their relationship to men, but not describing men by their relationship to women;
- ◎ referring to women as 'girls' but giving male figures the adult label, 'men';
- ◎ often using fixed collocations where the male referents occur first - as in 'he or she', 'husband and wife', 'men and women'.

Miller and Swift (1981) were advocating some practical reforms which consisted of trying to encourage communicators to think about the possible effects of their language uses. To this extent, they were aiming to make representations of men and women fairer and more equal. But the notion that language could be made to represent men and women equally is not an idea that has gained universal acceptance.

The radical tradition

A feminist tradition very different from that represented by Miller and Swift has rejected the idea that language can be 'improved' by making small adjustments such as those proposed above. This more radical tradition has maintained that women have been forced to use a language which is not their own and which they therefore cannot use to express their experiences effectively: in other words, they have been forced to see the world through male eyes. This is because women have been excluded historically from the production of powerful public discourses. Smith (1978: 281–82) describes this process:

> This is how a tradition is formed. A way of thinking develops in this discourse through the medium of the printed word as well as in speech. It has questions, solutions, themes, styles, standards, ways of looking at the world. These are formed as the circle of those present builds on the work of the past. From these circles women have been

excluded ... they have never controlled the material or social means to the making of a tradition among themselves or to acting as equals in the ongoing discourse of intellectuals.

Activity: gaps and distortions

What is meant by 'ways of looking at the world' (in the quotation above) could easily take another whole book to explore. But here are some examples for you to think about, discuss and research. You could start this process by doing some investigations of vocabulary in any dictionaries, etymologies and textbooks you have to hand. The examples below are all from academics in different subject areas researching ideas about sexual experiences, and many are quoted in Spender (1980). They are all claiming that our language, as it exists at present, gives men and women very different stories about sexual behaviour and about the importance of their sexual experiences. How far do you think their ideas are valid?

◎ there is no term for normal sexual power in women, to match the term 'virile' or 'potent' for men. There are only the extremes of 'frigid' and 'nymphomaniac';

◎ terms for sexual intercourse – such as 'penetration' – are invariably male-oriented; if women had named the same thing, the English language might use the term 'enclosure' instead;

◎ why is the term 'rape' not considered taboo, while another four-letter word describing female genitals is often considered the strongest taboo word in the English language?;

◎ there are large discrepancies between the numbers and types of terms available to label women as promiscuous – such as 'tart' and 'slag' – and those available to label men;

◎ many medical textbooks link female genitals with reproduction (i.e., focus on ovaries and womb rather than clitoris) but male genitals with sexual intercourse and pleasure. For example, Dorling Kindersley's *Children's Dictionary* (on CD-ROM, 1996) has the following for male and female genitals:

penis: the part of a man's body that he uses to urinate or to have sex.
vagina: the passage that connects the outside of a woman's body to her womb.
clitoris: no reference.

    ⊚   while female sexuality is either described in negative ways or not described at all, male sexuality is the basis of some very positive and high status words. For example, the words 'seminal', 'seminar' and 'disseminate' have the same derivation as that of the term 'semen'.

The terms above are all examples of what the poet Adrienne Rich (1979) has called 'telling it slant' – the way in which many women, according to some radical feminist critics, have had to define their experiences in spite of the available language, and not through it. For such critics, changing language in the way that Miller and Swift (1981) advocate is pointless, because it's just tinkering at the edges. A radical view would see the whole language system as **phallocratic** and **patriarchal**, and would say that we need to unpick all our social discourses to reveal the thinking that lies behind them. This view doesn't seek to patch up an imperfect language system, but to challenge and disrupt uses of language that are not normally seen as problematic, in order to show up our social power-lines.

    Below are two examples of radical writers whose aim is to challenge our thinking by inventing new terms or by giving existing ones new meanings. It's important to realise that these writers are engaged in a very different task from Miller and Swift. For a start, these radical writers are not suggesting that the terms they invent should be part of our everyday language use: their aim is to raise our consciousness rather than help us write an everyday text. Also, both writers are working with creative licence to create types of narrative whose purpose is to propose alternative 'realities'. To this extent, they are closer to writers of fiction such as George Orwell, who invented new types of language in *1984*, or to Anthony Burgess, who did the same in *A Clockwork Orange*.

Writer 1

Suzette Hayden Elgin, an anthropologist as well as a novelist, invented a new language called 'Laadan' in her *Native Tongue* novels (1985, 1987). Elgin (1981) uses new lexical items to encode what she sees as common female experiences. Here are some examples:

> *acanthophile* A woman who repeatedly chooses to form relationships with persons who abuse or neglect her, despite apparent unhappiness each time. (From Gr. *acanthos*, 'thorn').
> *bordweal* An artificial barrier raised to keep women out of things such as an irrelevant height requirement. (From O.E., *bord-weal*, 'a wall of shields').

to granny To apply the wisdom and the experience of the elderly woman to any situation.

scratscrak A night spent tending children, the sick, the helpless, while male members of the household sleep peacefully through it all; an ugly word coined to be ugly. You'll have no trouble pronouncing it.

Writer 2

Mary Daly, a feminist theologian, wrote (with Jane Caputi) an 'alternative' dictionary, *The Websters' First New Intergalactic Wickedary* (1987). Here are two entries from it:

> *Spinster n*: a woman whose occupation is to Spin, to participate in the whirling movement of creation; one who has chosen her Self, who defines her Self by choice neither in relation to children nor to men; one who is Self-identified; a whirling dervish, Spiraling in New Time/Space.
> *Old Maid n*: a Crone who has steadfastly resisted imprisonment in the Comatose State of matrimony.

The 'wickedary' is a playful exercise, but it has a serious purpose – to raise awareness of how dictionary compilers have acted as 'authorities' in traditionally defining the sexes, and particularly the female sex, in very restricted and potentially damaging ways. Webster's is a very well-known and long-standing American dictionary; Daly's *Websters' Wickedary* spins several webs of new associations, inventing new terms and reclaiming many old ones, particularly those that have traditionally been used negatively to refer to women, such as 'crone', 'battle-axe', 'hag', 'nag', 'gossip' and 'witch'. She also divides existing words up in a new way and gives them a new morphological structure. Here are some examples, illustrating all these strategies:

> *Crone-logical adj*: be-ing in accordance with the clarifying logic of Crones; able to see through man's mysteries/misteries; marked by a refusal to be side-tracked by the tedious, tidy, tiny, and ill-logical steps of male methodology/methodolatry.
> *olds, the*: the same old stories: patriarchal 'news' as reported/distorted by the assorted officious olds agencies and disseminated in the daily oldspapers.

phallosophy n: inflated foolosophy: 'wisdom' loaded with seminal ideas and disseminated by means of thrusting arguments.

Syn-Crone-icities n: 'coincidences' experienced and recognised by Crones as Strangely significant.

the/rapist n: a psycho-ologist who practises what he preaches/teaches.

It is unlikely that you will have had any of the terms from the radical tradition on your original list of 'politically correct' items. But you may have done, because when books such as those above have been reviewed, items of language have sometimes been picked out and ridiculed by right-wing commentators who have pretended to believe that the writers were advocating the use of these terms in everyday discourse.

The language is under attack!

Objectors to language reform often lump together all the different sorts of language examples we have looked at, and call them examples of 'politically correct' language.

The suggestion is typically that the language is adhering to a political line which either favours disadvantaged groups, or which does them a disservice by inventing new terms instead of campaigning for equality in more effective and practical ways. In the process, the language system itself is often characterised as being under attack and in need of protection from new and dangerous forms of 'thought police'. These ideas will be considered one by one in this final section.

The thought police are coming

The idea of 'interfering' with language is an interesting one, because it assumes that language is naturally occurring rather than humanly constructed. It is easy to feel as though the origins of language were far in the past, and that the process of meaning creation is over and done with. Yet this process is going on all the time, under our noses. Here is one example, taken from Spender (1980: 164–65):

An experiment was conducted to compare male and female visual perception, where subjects were asked to look at a picture and could either separate the stimulus (an embedded figure) from the background or else see the stimulus and background as a whole picture. It was found that men were more likely to do the former, and women the latter.

The scientists conducting the experiment called the male behaviour 'field independence', and the female behaviour 'field dependence'. Spender asks what the difference in connotations would have been if the male behaviour had been described as 'context blindness' and the female behaviour 'context awareness'. Spender's terms would have fitted the experimental results just as well, but the connotations of male and female behaviour would have been very different.

Cameron (1995) suggests that the strength of objections to language changes may be associated with the fact that the objector is being forced to see his or her own language use as not universally accepted – that others have a different understanding of terms. This means that there is no 'safe' place – whether you say, 'chairman', 'madam chairman', 'chairperson' or 'chair' says something about you. 'Politically correct' language causes anxiety because it is 'a challenge to the whole idea of a universal and neutral language' (ibid.: 120).

Just what are you supposed to call them these days?

One frequent aspect of complaint about 'politically correct' language is that the terms that are acceptable are constantly changing. For example, should you say 'homosexual' or 'gay'? Is black still OK, or should it be 'people of colour'? Should it be 'mixed race' or 'bi-racial'? Are people in wheelchairs 'disabled' or 'wheelchair-users'? Are older people 'elderly' or 'senior citizens'? Are children with learning problems 'slow learners' or 'children with special needs'?

If you stand back from these terms, you will notice that there are hidden categories above, categories that are not mentioned in all this labelling. Those are the categories that represent the norm in each case: heterosexual, white, pure (as opposed to 'mixed'), mono-racial, able-bodied, young, normal learners. An important point to note, then, is that the process of labelling is a process of identifying difference from a norm and that objectors to change often belong to that invisible and unstated norm from which others are judged as deviant. This idea of categorisation and norm-construction was at the core of the work you did in Unit three. While those labelled are constantly being re-labelled because their new labels attract negative meanings, people who represent the 'norm' are never labelled at all – they are just 'people'.

Another important aspect to note is that changes in terms are not arbitrary or whimsical, but happen for good reasons. For example, consider these labels, which were attached to the groups above in previous years (in some cases, until quite recently):

queer
nigger
half-caste
half-breed
cripple
old age pensioner
mentally retarded

More recent changes – say, from 'black American' to 'African American' – also signify important shifts in perspective. This particular change alters the label from one of physical appearance and skin colour to ideas about heritage and culture. Consider the uproar that would ensue if someone suggested that Italians, Spanish and British people should all be lumped together under the label 'whites'. Consider the fuss at present about even being called 'European'. Sometimes, labels are rejected or thought of negatively because of the history of their invention and because of who has 'owned' the term. For example, the term 'homosexual' came from the days when the medical profession saw being gay as a pathological illness, whereas 'gay' is a term invented by gay people themselves.

Naming and reclaiming

Cameron suggests that the whole phenomenon of language reform challenges the majority power group's assumptions that they can define the world: 'At stake is a power structure in which certain people, often without being conscious of it, just assume the right to tell other people who they are' (1995: 144).

Changes in naming can also represent a group's reaction to its own label, to being given an identity by others. This can mean that, sometimes, a group will defiantly use a label that has been given as a negative representation, and turn that label into something positive. You saw this process in Mary Daly's use of the term 'crone'.

The reclaiming of terms can be seen as a form of group resistance, but it gives objectors to language reform further grounds for complaint: why should Daly and her colleagues be able to use the term 'crone' to each other, thereby appearing rather 'politically incorrect', when men have been told for years that this is an insulting term that is off-limits?

Political correctness and context

The reclaiming of terms by groups who have been traditionally labelled in negative ways undoubtedly makes life more difficult for those in majority power groups who have not been on the receiving end of such labels. That is partly the point of the exercise. So while women can address each other affectionately as 'girls', while gay men and women have developed new forms of analysis called 'Queer Theory', and while young black men might use 'nigger' to each other as a positive form of address, the use of these terms to these groups by people who are outsiders produces a very different set of connotations. Who is talking and to whom, plus all the other contextual factors of language use, make up what we call the 'meaning' of any term.

Group resistance to forms of negative labelling has arguably forced everyone to do more thinking about the language they use. If the tradition of complaint about 'political correctness' has arisen because of the discomfiture of majority power groups, then this looks like a very positive development.

Summary

In breaking down what is meant by the term 'political correctness', three different types of language use were identified as commonly being labelled under this heading:

◎ new language items that are mythical, devised for purposes of satire by right-wing commentators;
◎ new language items that have been suggested by liberal critics, for use in real contexts;
◎ new language items that have been created by radical critics, in order to reveal prevalent ideologies, but not necessarily for everyday use.

It was suggested that the term 'political correctness' itself was typically used by people who object to language reform *per se,* and who would classify all the examples above as wrongful and misguided uses of English.

This unit went on to look at particular aspects of the 'political correctness' debate:

◎ the idea of the language system as under attack by new controlling forces;
◎ the idea of the rapid changes in terms;
◎ the idea of resistance and disruption.

Extension

1 Do a survey in order to discover what people understand by the term 'political correctness'. You could use some of the different examples of terms quoted in this unit, and get them to classify terms they think are acceptable, or not.

2 Look up the term 'political correctness' in a newly published dictionary, to see if it is defined and if so, how. Collect any examples of articles about this issue in newspapers — for example, from the letters pages.

3 Review Miller and Swift's (1981) areas of language use that need attention. Focus on one or two areas and research current usage in texts of your choice.

4 Research language use about sexual experiences. For example, you could look at advice books aimed at teenagers, or pamphlets on sex education, or at problem pages in magazines. You could also investigate medical textbooks, contemporary and old.

5 Make up some new terms for experiences that you don't think get encoded. Here are some ideas: always having to go to the bar in a pub; being flattered into doing menial jobs like washing up or ironing because 'you do them so well', etc.

Gender and speech styles

We appear to have many ideas about how men and women use language, and in particular, how they *differ* in their language use. One very general question to ask straight away is why we are so interested in difference rather than similarity. This is not an easy question to answer, but it is something that you need to have in the back of your mind throughout this unit. It has probably occurred to you already, during your work in earlier units, but the quest for 'difference' seems to loom particularly large when male and female speech styles are under consideration. So, for example, here are the titles of two of the most commercially successful books of the 1990s about male and female communication and language:

> *Men are from Mars, Women are from Venus*
> *You Just Don't Understand: Men and Women in Conversation*

Do you think the following invented titles could have been best-sellers too?:

> *Women and Men are both from Jupiter*
> *I Know Just What You Mean: Women and Men in Conversation*

Difference is big news in the popular press and in magazines, too. You only have to look as far as the latest feature in *GQ* or *Cosmopolitan* on how to interpret the language of your partner, to find male and female 'versions' of language treated as though they were mutually unintelligible foreign languages. Are they really, or does treating them in this way make for good media copy?

The aim of this unit is to help you explore the whole idea of male and female 'difference' in language use. In order to do this, you will need to take in something of the history of research on gender and speech styles, because there has been a considerable amount of research done, and because academic ideas have changed significantly over the years. Also, the academic world, however much we might like to think otherwise, is part of society and, as such, is itself subject to gender stereotyping. Because of the need to cover a lot of ground, you will find that the style in this unit is less interactive than that of the other units in this book. But it is hoped that as a result of working through the unit, you will have an increased awareness of the thinking that you yourself bring to any research that you do, as well as an ability to be more critical of the research findings of others.

Folklinguistics

How a Lady Should Behave Out of Doors

In her behaviour out of doors, the gentlewoman is quiet and unassuming. She shuns any exaggeration of dress and fashion which would make her conspicuous; it is not her aim to attract the eye of the crowd, but to escape its notice. She does not sweep the pavement with trailing skirts or address her friends in loud tones. Neither does she attract attention by her boisterous laughter. The aim of the gentlewoman is to escape notice out of doors; that of the ill-bred woman to attract it. Therein lies the difference.

(*The Woman's Book: Contains Everything a Woman Ought to Know*,
Jack and Strauss, 1911: 327).

The first thing to explore is the extent to which we have embedded concepts in our culture about the way men and women speak, or the way they *should* speak. Because language is a form of behaviour, ideas about the language that is appropriate for men and women often find expression in books of social etiquette, such as the above. Actually, that's not quite true. It would be more accurate to say that social etiquette books have always dealt more with female behaviour, as male behaviour has traditionally been seen as the norm and in need of no particular advice or attention.

As well as the prescriptions and proscriptions of advice books, we also have popular sayings about male and female language, such as 'nice girls don't swear', and 'swearing like a trooper'. In these examples, the nature of the language remains unspecified because we rely on shared linguistic and cultural knowledge to fill in the gaps. For example, we know that the type of swearing the trooper (foot-soldier, male by default) is going in for is not going to be along the lines of 'oh dear' or 'oh bother'; equally, we know that 'nice girls don't swear' really means 'nice girls don't use four-letter words' and that the word 'nice' refers to public reputation – girls who are rated as respectable – rather than individual personality.

But even where we don't have expressions referring specifically to the language of women and men, you don't have to work very hard to pull up a host of associations about talk and gender. And here, too, we are dealing with hidden assumptions about male and female linguistic behaviour. For example, if someone said a woman was 'talking like a lady' or 'talking in a ladylike way', what might the speaker be implying? How might that differ from 'talking like a woman', or even 'talking like an old woman'? What about 'she's got a mouth like a fishwife'? What might someone mean if they referred to 'men's talk', 'bloke-ish talk', or 'laddish talk'?; and how about 'women's talk' or 'girl talk'? In Unit two, we focused particularly on the connotations of words, and Unit three explored ideas about norms and stereotyping. Here we are looking at the stereotypical connections we make between speech styles and gender (plus other social dimensions – for example, ideas about social class and age are clearly at work in many of the expressions quoted so far). When beliefs are encoded in language in the form of popular sayings, this is often called '**folklinguistics**' – popular beliefs about language. The idea is that such sayings are a bit like proverbs in being part of the cultural luggage we inherit from our community as we acquire language. The term 'folklinguistics' sounds rather quaint, conjuring up ideas of rustic life and folk dancing. But, as you'll see, popular beliefs about language are certainly not harmless.

Note: there are several activities to follow, after which there is an overall commentary.

Activity

Explore the possible connections between the folklinguistic expression 'nice girls don't swear' and the newspaper article overleaf. The article itself is confusing in its description of events, but what do you make of the way the crime is reported, particularly in the wording of the headline?

87

WOMAN'S WORDS 'TOO MUCH' FOR SOLDIERS

The language of a woman soldier said to have been raped by a gang of paratroopers was too much for at least two other men, Winchester Crown Court was told yesterday.

The two soldiers gave evidence in the trial at which 13 members of the Parachute Regiment deny raping or indecently assaulting a woman soldier, aged 23, in the paratroops barracks at Bulford camp, Wiltshire, last November.

One said he was awoken from his sleep by shouting and a woman's scream. He looked out of his door, saw a bare-legged woman and some soldiers in a corridor. 'I thought trouble was coming so I left', he said.

The case continues.

(*The Guardian*, 1990)

Activity

Think about and discuss the expressions referred to on the two previous pages. The expressions are a mixture of well-known sayings (such as 'nice girls don't swear') and hypothetical utterances (such as 'talking like a lady'). Regardless of how common the expression is, this activity centres on the same question: what might each expression reveal about our culturally embedded ideas on gender and talk? Here are the expressions again:

Swearing like a trooper
Nice girls don't swear
Talking in a ladylike way
Talking like a woman
Talking like an old woman
She's got a mouth like a fishwife
Men's talk
Bloke-ish talk
Laddish talk
Women's talk
Girl talk

It might be helpful to work through this activity in two stages, first thinking about the language itself, then the supposed speakers.

The language
What kind of talk is being suggested in each case? For example, is the focus on:

◎ vocabulary items?
◎ the topics covered in the talk?
◎ the way the talk is managed by the participants?
◎ accent?

The speakers
How are men and women being represented? For example, is the focus on their:

◎ social class?
◎ age?
◎ sexual behaviour or sexuality?
◎ conformity to an ideal of masculinity/femininity?

Taking expressions such as the above out of context can be a starting point for thinking about our cultural values, but meaning can only be fully determined in context – in other words, by thinking about who is speaking, and where, and for what purpose. With this idea in mind, to what extent might the meaning of the expressions you have been studying be changed by who is saying them, and in what context?

Finally, add any further items that you think reveal our ideas about male and female language styles. You might also play around with the expressions above and see what effects are produced by making them refer to the opposite sex. Here are some examples:

Swearing like a nursery nurse
Nice boys don't swear
Boy talk
Talking like a gentleman
He's got a mouth like a fishhusband
Talking like a man/an old man

Activity

Read the poem by Liz Lochhead. What is this poem saying about male and female speech styles?

Men Talk (Rap)
Women
Rabbit rabbit rabbit women
Tattle and titter
Women prattle
Women waffle and witter

Men Talk. Men Talk.

Women into Girl Talk
About Women's Trouble
Trivia 'n' Small Talk
They yap and they babble

Men Talk. Men Talk.

Women gossip Women giggle
Women niggle-niggle-niggle
Men Talk.

Women yatter
Women chatter
Women chew the fat, women spill the beans
Women ain't been takin'
The oh-so Good Advice in them
Women's Magazines.

A Man Likes A Good Listener.
Oh yeah
I like A Woman
Who likes me enough
Not to nitpick
Not to nag and
Not to interrupt 'cause I call that treason
A woman with the Good Grace
To be struck dumb
By me Sweet Reason. Yes –

A Man Likes a Good Listener
A real
Man
Likes a Real Good Listener

Women yap yap yap
Verbal Diarrhoea is a Female Disease
Woman she spread she rumours round she
Like Philadelphia Cream Cheese.

Oh
Bossy Women Gossip
Girlish Women Giggle
Women natter, women nag
Women niggle niggle niggle

Men Talk.

Men
Think First, Speak Later
Men Talk.

(Liz Lochhead, *Dreaming Frankenstein*, Polygon Books)

Commentary

A common thread running through some of the data you have been studying is a connection between gender and social class. Both the terms 'lady' and 'gentleman' suggest privileged figures concerned with social etiquette and respectability within 'polite' society. The implication in the phrases 'talking like a lady/gentleman' compared with 'talking like a man/ woman' is that, regardless of gender, people lower down the social scale have 'worse' linguistic habits that their social 'betters'. It is no accident that it's the trooper who is seen as swearing profusely, rather than the brigadier or general, and the fishwife rather than the aristocratic lady.

However, 'lady' and 'gentleman' have had differing histories in terms of their connotations. While both terms still exist in the fixed phrase 'ladies and gentlemen', and as labels on toilet doors, the term 'lady', rather than 'woman', is often used as the equivalent of 'man', and 'gentleman' seems to be restricted in its usage. So, for example, children not looking where they are going will be told 'mind that lady', rather than 'mind that woman'. Feminist analysis has long explained this variation as the result of the way the term 'woman' has acquired negative connotations, so that 'lady' is seen as a 'polite' alternative. For many women, though, 'lady' is something of a false compliment, in having connotations of decorative ornamentation – an ineffectual figure not to be taken seriously, particularly in the workplace. So speaking in a 'ladylike' way may have similar connotations, of polite but trivial talk. Would this kind of talk (and talker) seem appropriate in a business negotiation?

Gender cuts across social class stereotypes in further significant ways, affecting women differently from men. In depictions of women, social class is often linked with sexual behaviour: in the text from the etiquette book, it is only the 'ill-bred' woman who 'attracts the eye of the crowd' by laughing and calling out. A 'lady' should be quiet and inconspicuous, not drawing attention to herself. 'Nice girls don't swear' tells us that if girls swear they might forfeit their good reputations: 'nice' in this phrase is not about being friendly or helpful, it is about being sexually chaste and therefore of a good 'class' of woman. The word 'nice' here is sexualised. So, if a woman swears – a very direct way of drawing attention to herself – she is not respectable, not a 'lady'. *The Guardian* article can be read in this way, too. The way the article is written (which is, presumably, a reflection of the way the defence case was presented in court) makes it unclear which was the crime: rape or a woman's language use?

Somehow it seems that a link is being made between the alleged rape and the woman's 'unacceptable' language – such bad language that even paratroopers found it 'too much'. One reading of this is that, because of her 'bad' language, she was not a 'nice' girl (i.e., she was a 'bad' girl) and therefore was not considered worthy of help from the 'two other men' who were not part of the alleged gang-rape. The implication from that is that she deserved what was happening to her. But even if you don't agree with this reading, there still needs to be some explanation of what relevance a woman's language use can possibly have to her being subjected to an alleged sexual attack.

But it is not simply the case that, while female behaviour is often constructed and interpreted in particular ways, men have freedom to define themselves in any way they want. There are both overt and covert messages about male linguistic behaviour, too. For example, that 'real men' (like troopers) swear a lot and use extreme words. In the reversed phrase, 'nice boys don't swear', 'nice boys' is an unusual collocation, showing us that the norm for masculinity (and therefore 'masculine' language) is 'not nice' – rough, tough, nasty, the stereotype of heterosexual maleness. In looking at types of talk, too, there are different ideas about the nature of men. For example, would 'bloke-ish' or 'laddish' talk encompass the idea of gay men as participants?

Male and female speakers seem to be characterised differently where age is concerned. At first sight, it looks as though an age range is being described, with 'girl talk', 'women's talk', and talking like an 'old woman'. But the age references are deceptive. For a start, 'old woman' is more likely to be a term used about men than women, with the suggestion of fussy behaviour, and on the principle that accusations of 'femaleness' are the ultimate insult to men – the same principle behind terms like 'sissy'. And references to 'girl' do not necessarily mean 'young woman', since adult women can often be referred to as 'girls'. Spender (1980) suggests that if you look at the way terms are applied to women, you may be under the impression that women never grow up, since they remain girls until they become 'old girls'.

Although we have ideas about the way the sexes talk encoded in our culture, that doesn't mean that words and phrases remain absolutely static or fixed in their meaning, regardless of who is saying them. For example, 'talking like a woman' could be intended to mean something very positive if used by a feminist speaker, while meaning something very negative if used by an anti-feminist. 'Talking like a man' would not necessarily be a compliment if the speaker had a misandrist (anti-male) view. But the fact remains that, while people have some room to manoeuvre and can reconstruct meanings consciously within their daily discourse, there are meanings that prevail in the wider culture through their constant circulation in particular and powerful domains. So, for example, 'talking like a man' is still likely to imply something a lot more positive and powerful than 'talking like a woman' in our culture's public discourses (McConnell-Ginet, 1998).

If the explanation above seems to you to suggest that we can hold two very different and somewhat contradictory ideas in our heads at once, then your reading is right. We might ourselves have had experience which leads us to a particular view, but that might be completely at odds with ideas that are in circulation in the wider culture. As individuals, we 'know' both. A concrete example is the stereotyping of occupations in 'swearing like a trooper/nursery nurse'. We may have met some rather foul-mouthed nursery nurses, and some very well-mannered troopers, but we will still know the traditional stereotypes of these figures. In the same way, the fact that we know men who gossip and nag, or women who are very forthright and assertive in conversation doesn't stop us from understanding the traditional stereotypes of male and female talk as the reverse of this pattern.

Liz Lochhead's poem adds a further dimension, and that is that the same behaviour by men and women can be labelled differently – men 'talk', while women 'gossip' and 'nag'. In talking about her poem on a BBC video (*The Language File: Nice Girls Don't Swear*), Lochhead explains that her take on this issue was ironic – she is not saying that this is what happens, she is saying that this is how society differentiates in a sexist way. However, she goes on to say that the poem has met with mixed responses when she has performed it in schools and colleges to students. On the one hand, some male listeners have not understood that she was being ironic, thinking she was simply describing 'reality'; on the other hand, some female listeners have said that they see the ways of talk attributed to women as a wide repertoire of talk styles that they were proud of, and that they rated their talk skills more highly than those of male speakers who have only one way of expressing themselves. This has connections with the idea of language reclamation that you studied in Unit four.

A history of research on gender and speech styles

There are comments about male and female language in our cultural written archives as far back as the Bible, but one of the first linguists to give the area the stamp of academic authority in modern times was Otto Jesperson, in his *Language: Its Nature, Development and Origin* (1922), which was a very influential and highly rated book for many years. His chapter on sex differences in language speaks volumes by its title: 'The Woman'. In other words, men are seen as the norm and women as departing from that norm in various ways - as being deviant. Jesperson pays most attention to vocabulary differences and despite having only anecdotal evidence for what he says, gives a long list of male and female lexical variations. However, more interesting than the actual examples are the generalised judgements that he makes about what these variations amount to. For example, women are seen as having limited vocabularies: 'the vocabulary of a woman as a rule is much less extensive than that of a man ...' They are also described as being rather delicate, easily offended and oblique:

> There can be no doubt that women exercise a great and universal influence on linguistic development through their instinctive shrinking from coarse and gross expressions and their preference for refined, and (in certain spheres) veiled and indirect expressions ...

Jesperson claims that men are the people who invent new terms, while women are innately conservative:

> men are the chief renovators of language ...

He also sees women as having a dulling effect on language use:

> Men will certainly with great justice object that there is a danger of
> the language becoming languid and insipid if we are always to con-
> tent ourselves with women's expressions and that vigour and vivid-
> ness count for something . . .

Early feminist critiques of language pointed to writers such as
Jesperson, and to earlier figures such as prescriptive eighteenth-century
grammarians, in order to show how stereotyped ideas about women's
language have been written into academic discourses as **received
opinion**. One such critique was Robin Lakoff's *Language and Woman's
Place* (1975).

Lakoff's central point was that women were socialised into sounding like 'ladies', which then in turn kept them in their place because
being 'ladylike' is a bar to being 'powerful' in our culture. This is because
power is associated with male behaviour and male discourse. In other
words, women were being trained to sound inferior. At the time, the idea
of women being in a no-win situation – if they talked like 'ladies' they
were seen as powerless and trivial, but if they talked like men they
were seen as unfeminine – struck a chord with many people, including
feminist researchers. But two aspects of this kind of approach led to some
unfortunate results, which are outlined below.

First, the idea above often ended up being interpreted as meaning
there was something wrong with the way women used language, so it was
women who needed to change their behaviour if they wanted access to
power. Associated with this was the idea that if their 'language problem'
was sorted out, then women would be given fairer treatment and would
somehow be more successful. This is not necessarily what Robin Lakoff
was herself saying in any direct way – remember that there is often a gulf
between the complexity of research findings and how those findings are
distilled in the wider culture. While research itself is often very revealing
about the thinking of the researcher, the way research is summarised and
reported is just as revealing about the values of the culture in and beyond
the academic world.

The idea that there might be something intrinsically wrong with
the language of a disadvantaged group (as opposed to something wrong
with our attitudes towards them) is now called the **deficit model** of
language. This term has been coined with the benefit of hindsight, but
it is a mistake to view such thinking as exclusively a thing of the past.

95

Activity

Discuss how the language of the following groups is thought about and described now in our culture. Is there any evidence that a deficit model of their language exists? (There is no commentary on this activity.)

- People with regional accents.
- Speakers using non-standard grammar (e.g. we was, I were, they ain't, I never done it).
- Writers using non-standard grammar.
- Speakers of Afro-Caribbean Patwa.

The idea of a deficit model of women's language has led to an array of courses designed for women to become more 'effective': for example, assertiveness-training or management-training courses for women, teaching them how to sound more authoritative and be taken more seriously. In short, an industry of language remediation has been making a good living out of the deficit idea. This also applies, of course, to other groups' so-called language deficiencies: think of speech-training courses where the norm is **received pronunciation** (RP), or literacy programmes that are sets of drills for Standard English. But a further aspect of language deficit work has arisen out of early books such as Robin Lakoff's, and that is work that has been very much within linguistic research itself. You might call this work 'deficit feature-spotting' because it has consisted of chasing small items of language that were seen by Lakoff as characterising female usage. Some examples are given below.

1   The use of terms relating to traditionally female work (such as working with fabrics) – for example, a greater range of terms for colours than men use (examples: aquamarine, fuchsia, lavender, etc., instead of more basic terms such as blue or red).
2   'Empty' adjectives such as 'charming', 'cute' (American English usage).
3   Intensifiers such as 'so', in phrases such as 'that's so good'.
4   The use of tag questions – where a statement is turned into a question by putting a tag on the end, as in 'the meeting is at eight o'clock, isn't it?'
5   Use of 'hedges' such as 'kind of' and 'you know'.

Nowadays, the idea of researching small items such as the above in terms of male and female usage is seen as rather dubious, for a number of reasons.

The 'so what?' criticism

So what if men and women use some aspects of language differently, particularly vocabulary? Wouldn't that be what you'd expect if men and women were told from an early age they should be interested in different areas? What is often more interesting than the supposed differences themselves are the conclusions that are drawn from such findings. For example, Jesperson quotes research where 25 university students were asked to write down 100 words as quickly as possible. It was found that many of the men's words related to the animal kingdom, while many of the women's words related to fabrics and food. The conclusions from this were that:

> In general the feminine traits are an attention to the immediate surroundings, to the finished product, to the ornamental, the individual, and the concrete; while the masculine preference is for the more remote, the constructive, the useful, the general and the abstract.
>
> (Ellis, 1904: 189)

While it takes something of an imaginative leap to get from the original examples to the summary, it seems bizarre that knowing the names of animals was seen as more 'constructive and useful' than knowing about fabrics and food!

The linguistic relativity criticism

Itemising language in this way suggests that a language feature has only one possible meaning and that the meaning is somehow contained in the structure. So, for example, Lakoff suggests that tag questions are signals of uncertainty, because they ask for reassurance. But what about the following phrases: are these expressions of uncertainty, just because they are tag questions?

> Nice day, isn't it?
> You won't do *that* again, *will* you?
> You're a nasty bit of work, aren't you?

Tag questions are complex items that can convey a range of different meanings where much depends on how they are said and the relationship between the interlocutors. In fact, shortly after the publication of Lakoff's book, two researchers (Dubois and Crouch, 1975) researched the use of tag questions in an academic setting and found that men used them more. Interestingly, the idea that men were therefore hesitant and lacking confidence didn't catch on.

The language context criticism

Language usage and how it is viewed are powerfully affected by context, including the setting and purpose of the interaction. Basing their work on Lakoff's idea that some aspects of women's language signal hesitancy, two researchers (O'Barr and Atkins, 1980) examined the use of hedging features (for example, 'sort of', 'kind of') in a courtroom setting, and found that people judged speakers who used such features as less convincing than those who didn't. The researchers concluded that there were certain linguistic features that marked someone's language as 'powerless' in some universal way. The problem was that they didn't take account of the fact that a courtroom setting demands certain kinds of language and if you pepper your utterances in that context with 'sort of's then you are bound to be seen as uncertain whereas in another setting you might not be seen in this way at all.

Linguistic developments

We now know considerably more about the way many aspects of spoken language work. As a result, some of the features previously considered 'empty' and redundant – such as 'sort of' – are now seen as fulfilling very important functions. For example, many features of so-called 'vague language', such as *'a bit of* lunch', 'twenty *or so*', 'shopping *and stuff*', *'about* forty' are understood as crucial aspects of interpersonal communication for everyone, allowing speakers to sound relaxed and informal (Channell, 1994).

The cultural diversity criticism

Much early feminist research was dominated by a white, middle-class, heterosexual, American point of view. In treating women as if they were all in one category, all sorts of other differences were made to disappear, making the research focus very narrow and the explanations of variation even narrower. For example, what kind of woman might use a very elaborate system of colour reference? A fashion designer or interior designer? How many working-class black women become interior designers?

From deficit to dominance: men behaving badly

Two influential later publications – Thorne and Henley's *Language and Sex: Difference and Dominance* (1975) and Dale Spender's *Man Made Language* (1980) shifted the focus away from women as somehow deficient users of language towards men as dominating and controlling both interactions with women and the language system itself. From these books, in both cases covering a wide range of different types of research, came ideas about such areas as topic control, interruptions and verbosity, where at least research used data from real speakers rather than intuitions about idealised male and female figures.

In the process, some features of language that had been suggested previously by Robin Lakoff as markers of female uncertainty were read in very different ways when looked at in the context of a real, mixed-sex interaction. For example, Lakoff claimed that women tend to use more question forms than men, making them seem less assertive than if they had used more outright statements. In Pamela Fishman's (1977) research, women did use more question forms than men, but this was because in the mixed-sex conversations she studied, they were often responsible for what is often termed 'small talk' – getting people (their male partners in this case) to open up and chat to them. Asking questions is then seen not as some universal feature of 'women's language', signalling uncertainty and powerlessness, but as part of the conversational labour women are often required to perform in their social role. This later research then had a more subtle reading of how men and women behave as a result of the roles they feel are their responsibility in interactions. This was making an important link between the features of language and their functions – the uses they are put to.

With responsibility come rights, and these two publications said much about how the linguistic rights of talk, topic control and turn-taking appeared to be distributed. For example, Zimmerman and West concluded, after studying 30 single-sex and mixed-sex conversations, that 'females are a class of speakers whose rights to speak appear to be casually infringed on by males' (1975: 125). This was because in the 11 mixed-sex conversations they studied, there were 48 interruptions, 98 per cent of these by men. They saw interruption as one of several ways male speakers used to get turns and establish the topics they wanted to talk about. The researchers concluded that 'males assert an asymmetrical right to control topics' (ibid).

While studies such as the above focused on some of the strategies used in interactions, others looked at ways of assessing talk quantitatively in order to explore the stereotype of women as the talkative sex. For example, Swacker (1975) asked men and women to talk into tape recorder and describe a set of pictures they were given. The male speakers spoke for three times longer than the females. In the meantime, commentators such as Dale Spender were offering explanations of the seeming mismatch between the supposed talkativeness of women in the popular imagination, and their relative silence in experimental situations: that while in research women were being measured against men, in 'folklinguistics' they are measured against silence, which is men's preferred state for women.

From dominance to difference

The kind of work done above was useful in looking at real speakers, and in looking at how discourse strategies such as interruptions can be used to gain control of interactions. In addition, Dale Spender's focus on our written archives of language, such as dictionaries and grammar books, revealed the extent to which language is a socially constructed system rather than some natural phenomenon, and therefore can be used by powerful groups to encode their own meanings. She showed that in some respects language is 'man made' in the sex-specific as well as generic sense.

However, there was still a level of generalisation in explanations which didn't fit with many people's experience of men and women. For example, a picture seemed to emerge of bullying men and meek, oppressed women in interactions and, when the language system itself was discussed, of men sitting round conspiring how to do women out of their linguistic inheritance. Also, there was still limited exploration of context and of informants' understanding of tasks in experimental settings. For example, in the verbosity experiment mentioned above, is it that men just always talk more than women, or might there be something in the test situation that influences men and women to behave in a certain way? If a researcher came into your study group and asked the male and female students to describe a set of pictures and record themselves on tape, would you consider the results to be an accurate reflection of how much your male and female classmates normally talk?

One of the biggest difficulties, though, was that cultural differences were still not being accounted for in having categories labelled just 'men' and 'women'. For example, in what Deborah Tannen calls 'high engagement' cultures, where speakers have a combative style as part of their cultural rules of interaction (she quotes her own Jewish culture as one example of this), interrupting and overlapping others' speech are a common feature of both male and female speech. So how could variations such as these be accommodated?

Tannen's work became commercially very successful with the publication of a book in 1991 called *You Just Don't Understand: Men and Women in Conversation*, which was mentioned at the beginning of this unit. This book conceived the idea of difference between men and women as cultural: in other words, it asks you to suppose that men and women come from different cultures in the sense that they grow up to have completely different ideas about themselves, about their expectations, about their place in the world, and about, therefore, what conversations are for. Men and women learn the rules for their own sex, and then when they interact with the opposite sex, cultural clashes can occur in the same way as they can when two speakers use different languages.

Tannen claims that there are two fundamental forces at work in social interactions; power and solidarity. We ask ourselves how much power we have in relation to the other person, and we also ask how close we are to them – how much solidarity or 'likemindedness' we have. In Tannen's view, men and women are trained to pay more attention to one or other of these dimensions, men monitoring their interactions for aspects of power, and women monitoring theirs for signals of solidarity or intimacy. We think that the rules for our own sex work across the sex divide, but they don't. So, as a result, we use the same language but we are reading the same interaction in different ways.

This approach entails a re-interpretation of many of those same aspects that were the focus for previous research. For example, if men are trained to be competitive and one such strategy is that of interruption, while women's socialisation has taught them that their role is to draw others out and establish rapport, then in mixed-sex conversations men's and women's **gender scripts** – the rules they would use for their own sex – are potentially in conflict, with resulting inequality. The difference with this interpretation is that it doesn't construct men as intentional bullies nor women as feeble victims. And our gender scripts can be analysed, understood, played with, changed and resisted.

One of the strong points of Tannen's approach is that it focuses on the thinking behind our linguistic behaviour, seeing our language use as a result of what we think we're doing when we have a conversation. In this respect, it owes much to Speech Act Theory, which saw language as performance – for example, asking, promising, apologising, and so on.

101

But Tannen's view is that the sexes may understand these various linguistic performances in different ways. For example, what do we think we are supposed to do when someone presents us with a problem – solve it or talk about it? Do we see conversation as exchanging information or as relating to the other person in some other way? How do we report back on an event, by giving the bare bones of the story, or by working it up into a fictionalised narrative, replete with juicy details? In which contexts do we feel able to talk a lot, and in which do we feel 'out of place' doing so? When we say 'sorry' are we expressing sympathy or confessing culpability? When we use reinforcements (saying 'yeah' or 'mm' when someone is speaking) do they mean 'I'm listening' or 'I agree with you'?

After difference

A shift in emphasis from 'dominance' to 'difference' has been liberating in some ways. For example, researchers have felt justified in looking at women's styles of language without starting from the view that they were either deficient or oppressed. This has meant that women could be thought of as successful language-users who have their own ways to be powerful. At the same time, the idea of men being a simple locus of blame has been dissipated.

However, there have been major criticisms of 'difference' theorists, not the least of which is that they overlook the larger socio-political context. So, for example, while it might be laudable to maintain that women are very skilled at particular types of talk and that they have their own ways of 'doing gender', this means very little if we don't pay attention to how talk is valued within the wider culture. So who speaks from the pulpit, from the benches of the law courts, within the institutions of government, from our newspapers? Who are the figures who give us learned opinion on science, industry, technology and finance? Which figures are dished up again and again on literary booklists and art catalogues? Who constructs the male and female 'voices' in advertising texts? How are male and female musicians – people who really do have a 'voice' – seen and talked about? In other words, as well as looking at gender in daily interactions, we should also have a bigger vision which examines what has been called 'women's silence' in the larger culture, which often means either invisibility, or marginalisation. If this doesn't happen, then work such as Tannen's becomes, as Cameron (1995) would claim, just another advice book for women on how to talk to your man. In this sense, it would fall into line with the extract from *The Woman's Book: Contains Everything a Woman Ought To Know*, quoted on p. 86.

Another, related, criticism of 'difference' theorists is that the sexes are in important ways very *unlike* different cultures. Although we may learn what are appropriate behaviours for our own sex, we also have ideas from very early on about the opposite sex. It's a bit like saying that if we start life with a regional accent we don't know about Standard English until we are fully grown. In looking at regional language, an important issue is how speakers negotiate their language use in the face of the existence of Standard English; in a similar way, if we take Tannen's idea of the sexes as different cultures, a crucial focus should be intercultural studies - where research asks questions about cultures in contact, not cultures in isolation.

Finally, a more contemporary view of gender sees variety within this dimension rather than as a single, solid identity. Gender does not exist in isolation from factors such as ethnic origin, social class, sexuality or age, and the same 'gender' template is likely to fit across these variations only with some fairly drastic distortions. So, rather than a notion of 'femininity' or 'masculinity', we should be thinking in the plural - of femininities and masculinities. This means that, rather than repeating the endless mantra 'women do this, men do that', we should be asking 'how does this group of men/women in this context enact their gender'?

Summary

This unit has explored some of society's embedded beliefs about the way men and women talk. Starting with everyday ideas encoded in popular sayings, the unit moved on to look at how the academic world has approached this topic in changing ways over the years.

Extension

1   Research how some of the expressions that you studied at the start of this unit are understood, by constructing a questionnaire and interviewing a range of informants.
2   In one of the extracts from Jesperson, he used the term 'instinctive' when discussing women's attitude to swearing:

There can be no doubt that women exercise a great and universal influence on linguistic development through their instinctive shrinking from coarse and gross expressions and their preference for refined, and (in certain spheres) veiled and indirect expressions . . .

This gives the impression that women somehow have a 'natural' disposition to dislike 'coarse and gross expressions'. The same idea is at work in the assumption by some men in contemporary culture that they need to apologise to women for swearing in their company: 'not in front of the ladies', 'pardon my French'.

Because female reactions to swearing are often written up as something to do with women's 'natural sensitivity', there is less examination of swear words from a semantic point of view. But if swear words are examined for their content as well as their function, we may have a different reading of women's reactions.

Read the article on 'the big C'. How far do you agree with the ideas put forward here about the way men and women relate to 'the big C'?

3   Research some of the different approaches taken in written academic material to male and female speech styles. Choose a particular type of material: for example, study packs aimed at primary or secondary school pupils; textbooks or academic journals aimed at older students. Try to decide which of the approaches outlined in this unit is being taken by the writer.

4   Research the way male and female speech styles are depicted in literary texts or in the popular media. Think about how you might make a comparative study: for example, a male compared with a female 'sleuth' in detective fiction; male and female characters in children's readers, comics or photostory features in magazines.

5   Conduct some interviews with male and female students in your study group (or another group of your choice – for example, younger schoolchildren) about their talk patterns. For example, when do they feel confident in talking and when not? Are there certain contexts for talk that appear to be more male- or female-dominated?

6   Tape a conversation involving a single-sex group, and explore what ideas the speakers are projecting about themselves as a result of the themes and ideas they are discussing and in terms of how they conduct the conversation. Think particularly in your account of their talk about the context of the conversation – for example, what is the setting? Does the talk have a particular purpose? What is the composition of the group? Are there ways in which your presence, and that of a tape recorder, might have affected the course of events?

7   Repeat the above, but with a mixed-sex group. After you have studied your data and come to some conclusions about the interaction, interview the participants to see what their own 'readings' were of the way the conversation went.

8   There have been varying accounts of male and female speech in

The Guardian Tuesday March 3 1998 · **5**

Joan Smith asks why all the fuss over one little four-letter word

The big C

When the writers of the Channel 4 series Mosley wanted to shock viewers in the final episode, they knew exactly what to do. They wrote a scene in which a prison guard, screaming at the jailed fascist leader, uses "the most reviled single utterance in the English language", according to scriptwriter Laurence Marks. In other words, the character calls him a vagina.

Funny business, this. The f-word has become so commonplace that it is now written out in full, without dashes or asterisks, in newspapers like the Guardian. This is not true of the other four-letter word, "an anatomical reference which will prove deeply offensive to women in particular", as the Mail on Sunday described it at the weekend, displaying a rare blend of coyness and political correctness.

You may, especially if you are a woman, feel uncomfortable about this blatant misogyny, which allows men to appropriate an important part of our anatomy and turn it into a vile insult — "a nasty name for a nasty thing" as a dictionary published in 1811 characterised it. But there is no doubt that the word has great force. "We did it because it is immensely powerful," Marks admits. Channel 4 has defended its use in an "adult programme", screened after the 9pm watershed, but the very fact that it is being discussed, before the programme has been shown, demonstrates that the decision to broadcast it is controversial.

Things were not always thus. The OED's earliest example of the word's use dates from around 1230, when the residents of Gropecunt-lane in London did not, apparently, lose sleep over the unusual name of the street where they lived. (They may have passed some happy hours in conjecture of its origin, but that is another matter.) In the 14th century, it was the standard word for the vagina; Chaucer employs it matter of factly in The Canterbury Tales, though he preferred an alternative spelling, "queynte". By Shakespeare's day, it was no longer used in polite company, although the dramatist inserted a sly pun in Hamlet, assuming his audience would pick up the reference to "country matters". In the 18th century, its use in print actually became illegal, the first conviction taking place in 1717.

So when did it acquire its power as the worst possible thing — much worse than "prick" — one human being can say to another? More to the point, why did it become so offensive? It is impossible not to make a link, as lexicographers and feminist writers have done, between the word's decline into obscenity and illegality, and fearful attitudes towards women and their sexuality.

An article in the Village Voice in New York in 1977 made this point vividly, arguing that using the word about a man "is to call him a woman: castrated". Early attempts in the 20th century to restore its anatomical meaning, notably by DH Lawrence and James Joyce, were problematic. Mellors, in Lady Chatterley's Lover, uses it as a term of endearment, but it is hard to imagine many women enjoying the experience of being crudely equated with their sexual organs.

This is not to say that women haven't been trying to reclaim the word — not an easy task when men continue to cherish its status as invective. They certainly don't like to hear it from a woman and a theatre group that called itself Cunning Stunts (try saying it quickly) caused consternation among male critics who feared, correctly, that something rather subversive was going on. So does its use on TV, assuming Channel 4 does not lose its nerve before Thursday, signify that the word has started on the long road, already travelled by fuck, towards frequent use, if not acceptability?

My guess is that there is a gender divide here, with some women eager to reappropriate it in protest against its anachronistic slur on female sexuality; some of my female friends use it quite deliberately when they talk about their own bodies. This is a far more effective way of removing its sting than flinging it about on Channel 4 and it makes me wonder what the lads will do if we succeed in taking away their worst insult. Perhaps it's time to start talking, *pace* Freud, about the terrible problems men have in overcoming their cunt envy?

terms of accent, particularly on how far the sexes approximate to prestige forms (for example, in the use of RP). Read the chapter entitled 'Language and Sex' in Trudgill's *Sociolinguistics* (1980), which claims that women's accents are often closer to RP than men of the same class. Then read a critique of this approach in Spender (1980: 36–38). Finally, read Milroy's *Language and Social Networks* (1987), which has very different findings and a different explanation of gender and accent variation. A review of all of these readings can be found in chapters 2 and 3 of Coates and Cameron (1988).

9   Research some talk on the Internet, for example, in chatrooms where the speakers' sex is not immediately obvious (and where people can 'impersonate' speakers of another sex). There are many possible questions to ask here, but a starting point might be to see if there are ways people are signalling aspects of gender in what they talk about and in the way they interact.

Reading positions

Much of this book has been concerned with understanding some important principles and concepts, without which the topic of language and gender can only be grasped in a superficial way. Because the focus has been on the thinking that lies behind language structures and use, there has been more emphasis on words and phrases than on whole texts. This final unit offers some starting points for integrating the work you have done on cognitive models and language items into the study of larger textual patterns. Further ideas for exploring this subject will be given in the Further Reading section.

Narrators and narratees

In the past, models of communication have sometimes appeared to suggest that communication is simply a matter of passing a message from A to B: A encodes a message which is decoded by B. This may be true for very simple signalling, such as Morse code, but most of the texts that are around us on a daily basis have much more complex **address relationships** than that.

For a start, writers often construct a **persona** to address us, and this persona establishes a kind of voice which, via the language of the text, addresses us in a certain way. This persona is called a **narrator**. A simple example of this might be a male writer who constructs a female narrator.

You were invited to think about this dimension in the 'Extension' section of Unit two. Another example might be an adult writer who constructs a child narrator. You can see this at work in Alice Walker's *The Colour Purple* (1983), where the narrator is a 14-year-old girl.

It is not only writers of fiction who use narrators. Any writer who is paying attention to how they are coming across is establishing a narrative voice. You become a certain kind of narrator when you write essays; we have constructed a narrative persona throughout this book. You might pause to think what that voice has been like - have we sounded friendly or hostile, confident or nervous, clear or muddled? However we have sounded, you have no way of knowing what we are really like.

Just as texts have narrators, so they also have narratees. Narratees are implied readers - the people who appear to be being addressed by the text. For example, in Alice Walker's novel, the narratee is God: the novel consists of the young narrator's letters to him. Our book here has implied readers - we have addressed this text to a set of imagined students who may or may not equate with the real readers. If we have been successful in our construction of narratees, then our imagined and real readers are one and the same thing. But that is by no means inevitable. For example, if you feel that this book is either way too difficult or else stating the obvious, then you as a real reader are very different from how we have imagined you.

Activity

Think about some novels you have read, and identify what kind of narrators were presented in the books. For example, was there just one narrator or more than one? Were the narrators male or female, old or young, black or white, standard English users or regional dialect users, drunk or sober, reliable or unreliable? Did they live in the present, or past? Were they likeable or hostile? Did they address you directly, or did they seem quite removed from the story? Did they seem in control of the story, or were they presented as being swept along by events?

When you have finished your brainstorm, use the material you have gathered to think about the idea of the narratee, and how that worked in the books you have remembered. This can be done because, for every characteristic of the narrator you have identified, there are implications for the narratee. For example, if there was more than one narrator, then the narratee is thought to need more than one perspective — why? If the narrator used regional dialect, what does that mean about the identity of the narratee? Conversely, if the narrator used standard English, what does that mean?

The texts in this unit are both advertisements, rather than novels. But the same dimensions of narrator and narratee apply. Although adverts are quickly read, they are often not an 'easy read' in analytical terms. In fact, many adverts present considerably more complex sets of address relationships than novels do.

One aspect of adverts that is worth particular attention is that of the narratee. Adverts differ from novels in that they are consciously targeted at particular groups, and often present idealised constructions of narratees. That is, they offer an image for certain readers to aspire to, and, in the process, they present a strong profile or identity for those readers to relate to, and for 'excluded' readers to observe. Also, because adverts need to establish a rapid relationship with readers, they often use highly interactive strategies - such as questions, and forms of direct address, like 'you'. These strategies imitate the speech context and simulate the notion of 'striking up a conversation'.

A further way for advertising copywriters to establish a strong narrative voice quickly and in a small textual space is to use forms of **intertextuality** - referring beyond the text to other well-known texts. Because intertextuality is all about cultural knowledge, our reading of adverts often requires us to make connections between the particular text in front of us and aspects of our social knowledge, invoking the cognitive models that were the focus for Unit three.

Activity

Read through the text, which is advertising a PlayStation game called 'Zelda – Ocarina of Time'.

- ◎ Describe the nature of the narrator and the narratee, thinking particularly about the constructions of gender in the text.
- ◎ Does this text use any of the strategies outlined above?
- ◎ Is there only one possible reading of this text, or are there alternative readings? If there are alternatives, what is the status of these alternatives?

Commentary

It is interesting that such a small amount of text can be so rich in implications, supporting the idea that adverts are very dense and complex.

Text: Zelda

> **ZELDA**
>
> Ocarina of Time
>
> Willst thou get the girl?
>
> Or play like one?

The narrator appears to be a voice from previous centuries, when 'willst' and 'thou' were in regular use. This is endorsed by the phrase 'Ocarina of Time', which connotes a time-travelling theme, and the image of the sword and shield, which look medieval – a time of fair maidens and jousting knights.

The narrator uses the interactive strategy of asking a question, which is the form of a challenge – will the narratee be up to the task? If so, the narratee will 'get the girl' – an intertextual reference to all those stories where the heterosexual hero wins the hand of the woman as his reward for brave deeds. This phrase could also be read as meaning 'defeat the girl' in the sense of defeating the female warrior figure, Zelda.

The narratee is constructed as male as a result of the features of language above, but also because of the suggestion that failure would equate with 'playing like a girl' – in male terms, playing feebly.

It is possible to carry out alternative readings of this text, to adopt different reading positions that disrupt a majority view. For example, you could see the narratee as a gay woman who also might be interested in 'getting the girl', and you could maintain that female readers in general might 'reclaim' the notion of 'playing like a girl', to mean playing with dexterity and intelligence, or by using superior verbal abilities. However, these readings would still have to exist alongside the more mainstream reading, the 'norm model': that where the narratee is constructed as a young male whose identity and skills are being defined by distinction from negative female qualities, and where failure in battle equates with a reduction in masculine prowess. You worked on this idea of mainstream and alternative readings for terms when you looked at the phrase 'talking like a woman' in Unit five.

If the narratee is being constructed as male, then we also need to ask: What happens to those readers who feel excluded by the address system in this text? Just because we feel we are not being addressed by a text, we don't stop reading it. What we do is observe the interaction that is taking place, and come to certain conclusions ourselves about the nature of the narratee. In other words, the text doesn't just represent a certain kind of masculine identity to male readers; it also suggests 'what men are like' to female readers – in this case, that they are sexist. The text also, of course, represents women to themselves as inadequate players, endorsing the stereotype of women as weak and unassertive. In this way, discourses of all kinds circulate ideas about the nature of all of us, regardless of whether we are part of the textual interaction or not.

Texts are not smooth and coherent entities where all the bits add up. Often they suggest contradictory things which mirror some of the contradictions in our culture. For example, at the same time as women are being constructed as feeble players in the text above, the narratee is being invited to fight against a female warrior, who represents a very different representation of femininity. How come Zelda isn't seen as 'playing like a girl'? If she was, it would be no heroic feat for our narratee to win the game.

The lesson to be learnt here is that texts don't necessarily have a unified message, nor do they need to be based on one cognitive model. So, for example, it is perfectly possible to have female Amazonian warriors and damsels in distress in the same piece of discourse, without that disjunction posing any problems for readers.

Text: 'Something for the weekend ladies?'

Now read through the advert for Town and Country gloves, and answer the same questions as those set for the previous text. Where much of the meaning of the previous text revolved around the meaning of the word 'girl', this text throws the term 'ladies' into relief. Just as the previous text suggested ideas about what men and women are like (in the words of Unit two, 'what men and women are for'), so does the text here. It also resembles the previous one in presenting a particular model of masculinity. (There is no commentary on this activity.)

Summary

This unit has provided a brief introduction to text analysis, applying to everyday texts some of the ideas from previous units about gender and connotations, cognitive models and social knowledge.

Extension

1   Collect some adverts where it seems as though the narrator and/or the narratee is one sex or the other. Explore, by analysing the texts, why you have come to these conclusions as a reader. If possible, try out the texts on other readers, to see if they agree with your conclusions. What are the implications of your findings?

2   Collect and analyse any other texts that you consider present a strong profile of the narratee. You might consider looking at male and female versions of the same genre – for example, problem pages in male and female magazines.

3   Collect some texts that use intertextuality in order to construct ideas about gender. This could range from references to well-known sayings to ideas about whole texts. An example of the former is this slogan from an advert selling a new vacuum cleaner: 'a giant leap for womankind'; an example of the latter might be an advert that imitates a text normally associated with male or female readers – e.g. a recipe, or a scientific report.

index of terms

This is a form of combined glossary and index. Listed below are some of the key terms used in the book, together with brief definitions for purposes of reference. The page references will normally take you to the first use of the term in the book, where it will be shown in bold.

address relationships   107
> The network of relationships in a text based on who appears to be talking, and to whom (see **narrator** and **narratee**).

anthropomorphism   10
> A view that an animal or an object has feelings like those of a human being. A similar term is 'personification'. From Greek *anthropos*, 'human', and *morphe*, 'form'.

antonyms   59
> Words that are opposite in meaning, such as 'clean' and 'dirty'.

arbitrary   7
> Random, unconnected. When applied to language, it suggests that there is no intrinsic connection between language and its **referents**.

cognition   48
> A broad term which covers the area of mental events; the processes, structures and events through which we perceive, interpret and behave in the physical and social world. This includes thinking, reasoning, knowledge, memory, perception, etc.

cognitive model   51
> A 'mental' concept or representation of the knowledge we have about everything - people, animals, objects, events, attitudes, emotions, etc. This even includes our understanding of physical things like gravity - what it is and how it works.

collocation   30
> The repeated occurrence of words in the company of others, sometimes even in a set order, for example, 'fish and chips', 'bed and breakfast', 'men and women'.

connotation   6
> A level of meaning which is based on the associations surrounding a word. For example, the word 'child' could suggest ideas of purity and innocence (see **denotation**).

deficit model   95
> A model which ascribes fault or the lack of ability in the group being referred to.

denotation   27
> The barest, dictionary definition of a word. For example, the denotation for

'child' would be 'young human being' (see **connotation**).

deviant 58

A person, event or behaviour which does not fit the **norm** or expectations, hence the phrase 'to deviate from the norm'. Often the term 'deviant' has negative connotations and is typically used to refer to people or things that go beyond or fall outside socially acceptable boundaries - for example, 'sexual deviance'.

discrimination 7

The process of making distinctions; the process by which we distinguish between objects, events, categories, etc.

euphemism 31

A polite alternative expression for an area that is considered taboo. For example, the phrases 'sleeping with' and 'making love' are euphemisms for sexual intercourse. The opposite of a euphemism is called a 'dysphemism'. This refers to a deliberately crude alternative, such as 'shag'.

fire 48

A technical term which describes the action of a nerve cell (**neurone**) when it communicates or passes a chemical signal to other nerve cells. Firing involves an electrical impulse which triggers the release of a chemical messenger (a neurotransmitter).

folklinguistics 87

Ideas about language encoded in popular sayings such as proverbs.

gender scripts 101

The idea that the sexes adopt roles that are deemed appropriate to their sex, and express these roles in broad aspects of behaviour, rather as actors who have learnt roles and lines for performance.

generic reference 61

The ability of a term to refer generally.

hyponyms 55

Members of a category. For example, 'apple' and 'pear' are hyponyms of the category 'fruit'.

identity 34

The sense we have of our self and others as individuals and group members, and the 'story' or version of the individual that is portrayed and perceived.

ideology 54

A system of beliefs and ideas characteristic of a society, group or individual. This system influences thinking and explanations, and determines policies and practices.

intertextuality 109

The way in which one text echoes or refers to another text. Intertextuality can operate at many different levels, from single words or phrases to whole genres of text.

marking 47

The process or act of signalling an alternative meaning to 'normal', signalling a specific meaning which would otherwise be missed or incorrectly understood.

metaphor 6

A word or phrase which establishes a comparison or analogy between one object and idea and another. For example, saying that a woman has been 'left on the shelf' draws a comparison between women and saleable commodities.

metonymy 18

Often seen as a type of metaphor, metonymy refers to objects or ideas by using features often associated with them. For example, saying 'suits' instead of 'businessmen' in a sentence such as 'Two suits came into the room.'

modifier 32

A word or phrase which adds more detail (or modifies) another element. For examp[le], in the phrase 'male nurse', the adjective 'male' modifies the noun 'nurse'.

morphology 61

The different structural elements that are combined to form words. For example, in the word 'spinster' there are two morphemes, 'spin' (in the sense of cloth) and 'ster', which means 'female doer of action'. So a spinster was originally a female spinner of yarn. The morpheme 'ster' can be seen in some surnames, such as Baxter ('bakster' - female baker) and Brewster (female brewer).

narratee 38

The implied reader of a text. The identity of the narratee is established by sets of assumptions in the text about what the person reading it is like.

narrator 107

The person in a text who appears to be addressing the reader.

neurones 48

The cells of the nervous system (including the brain and spinal cord) which communicate or transmit information around the body.

norms 56

A rule or standard shared by a group of people which are held or believed to be the most common, frequent or acceptable, and which are used to guide behaviour and make judgements, decisions, etc.

[patri]archal 77

[Ma]le-controlled. The literal [mean]ing of 'patriarch' is 'head [of fa]mily unit'. The term [refers to the] way men have tra[ditionally be]en the head of the h[ousehold], and the way in which pr[op]erty laws and naming conventions have traditionally followed the male line of inheritance.

persona 107

A constructed figure, a fictionalised characterisation.

phallocratic 77

Male-centred, and/or the idea that the male sex is superior. From Latin *phallus*, 'penis'.

pronoun reference 16

This is an aspect of cohesion, or the way in which texts are woven together, particularly across sentence boundaries. Pronoun reference is the linking together of pronouns with other linguistic items. In the following example, the pronoun 'he' links back to the proper noun 'Bill': 'I went to work yesterday and saw *Bill. He* was looking very tanned.'

prototype 57

A type of cognitive model which represents the typical or ideal defining characteristics of a category.

received opinion 95

Views which are held as correct by the more powerful groups within an establishment.

received pronunciation 96

A social class accent which was officially 'received' in royal circles (hence the name), and which has traditionally been seen as prestigious.

referent 31

An object, person or idea being referred to.

salient 8

Meaningful, important, relevant, pertinent or requiring (cognitive) attention.

sex-specific reference 61

The way in which a term refers specifically to one sex or the other.

socialisation 34

The process of internalising our society; that is the process by which we learn a society's rules, roles and values so that we become a part of society and society becomes a part of us. For example, learning about how and when to be polite or that we shouldn't hit other people.

social knowledge 34

All the things we 'know' about our society, other societies and the physical world – how it works and everything in it (people, behaviour, objects, events, etc.). This is one of the products of socialisation.

stereotyping 47

The use of a simplified model where fixed characteristics are applied to individuals on the basis of their group membership.

suffixes 61

Elements that are added to the ends of words. For example, adding 'ette' to 'cigar' produces 'cigarette', 'a small cigar'. Elements such as 'dis' and 'un' that go on the front of words are called 'prefixes'.

urban myths 70

Contemporary stories, often with an urban setting and involving gruesome events, which tellers claim are true, but which turn out to be fictional.

references

Amis, M. (1997) *Night Train* (Jonathan Cape, London).

Bodine, A. (1975) 'Andocentrism in prescriptive grammar: singular "they", sex-indefinite "he", and "he or she",' *Language in Society*, 4, pp. 129-46. Reprinted in D. Cameron (ed.) *The Feminist Critique of Language: A Reader* (Routledge, London), pp. 124-38.

Cameron, D. (1995) *Verbal Hygiene* (Routledge, London).

Channell, J. (1994) *Vague Language* (Oxford University Press, Oxford).

Coates, J. and Cameron, D. (1988) *Women in their Speech Communities* (Longman, Harlow).

Coward, R. (1984) 'The sex life of stick insects', in R. Coward, *Female Desire* (Paladin, London).

Crowther, B. and Leith, D. (1995) 'Feminism, language, and the rhetoric of television wildlife programmes', in S. Mills (ed.) *Language and Gender: Interdisciplinary Perspectives* (Longman, Harlow).

Crystal, D. (1987) *The Cambridge Encyclopedia of Language* (Cambridge University Press, Cambridge).

Daly, M. and Caputi, J. (1987) *Websters' First New Intergalactic Wickedary of the English Language* (The Women's Press, London).

Dorling Kindersley Children's Dictionary (1996) (Dorling Kindersley, London). Available as CD ROM.

Dubois, B. and Crouch, I. (1975) 'The question of tag questions in women's speech: they don't really use more of them, do they?', *Language in Society*, 4, pp. 289-94.

Elgin, S. (1981) 'Some proposed additions to the glossary of needed lexical items for the expression of women's perceptions'. *Lonesome Node* 1, no. 1. [A range of Elgin's work is discussed in R. Bailey (1991) *Images of English: A Cultural History of the Language* (Cambridge University Press, Cambridge).]

Elgin, S. (1985) *Native Tongue* (Women's Press, London).

Elgin, S. (1987) *Native Tongue II* (DAW Books, New York).

Ellis, H. (1904) Cited in Jesperson, O. (1922) *Language: Its Nature, Development and Origin* (Allen & Unwin, New York).

Fishman, P. (1977) 'Interactional shitwork', *Heresies: A Feminist Publication on Arts and Politics*, no. 2, May, pp. 99-101.

Harvey, K. (1997) 'Everybody loves a lover', in K. Harvey and C. Shalom (eds) *Language and Desire* (Routledge, London).

Herriman, J. (1998) 'Descriptions of *woman* and *man* in present-day English'. *Moderne Språk*, XCII (2), 136-42.

Horwood, F.C. (ed.) (1971) *A.E. Housman: Poetry and Prose, A Selection* (Hutchison, London).

Hudson, J. (1999) Personal correspondence.

Jack, F.B. and Strauss, R. (1911) The Woman's Book: Contains Everything a Woman Ought to Know (T.C. & E.C. Jack, London).

Jesperson, O. (1922) *Language: Its Nature, Development and Origin* (Allen & Unwin, New York).

Jones, M. (1999) Personal correspondence. University of Nottingham.

Khosroshahi, F. (1989) 'Penguins don't care but women do: a social identity analysis of a Whorfian problem', *Language in Society*, 18, pp. 505-25.

Lakoff, G. (1987) *Women, Fire and Dangerous Things: What Categories Reveal about the Mind* (University of Chicago Press, Chicago).

Lakoff, R. (1975) *Language and Woman's Place* (Harper and Row, New York).

Lamb, C. (1980) *Seduction* (Harlequin Mills & Boon Ltd., Richmond).

Leonard, E. (1992) *Rum Punch* (Dell Publishing, New York).

Lochhead, L. (1986) *Dreaming Frankenstein* (Polygon).

McConnell-Ginet, S. (1998) 'The sexual (re)production of meaning: a discourse-based theory', in D. Cameron (ed.) *The Feminist Critique of Language* (Routledge, London).

Miller, C. and Swift, K. (1981) *The Handbook of Non-Sexist Writing* (The Women's Press, London).

Milroy, L. (1987) *Language and Social Networks* (Blackwell, Oxford).

Morgan, G. (1986) *Images of Organization* (Sage, London).

Ng, S.H. (1990) 'Language and Control', in H. Giles and W.P. Robinson (eds) *Handbook of Language and Social Psychology* (John Wiley & Sons Ltd., Chichester).

O'Barr, W. and Atkins, B. (1980) '"Women's language" or "powerless language"?' in S. McConnell-Ginet, N. Furman and N. Borker (eds) *Women and Language in Literature and Society* (Praeger, New York).

Policy Studies Institute (1989) Cultural Trends (Policy Studies Institute, London).

Rich, A. (1979) *On Lies, Secrets and Silence* (Norton, New York), p. 208.

Shalom, C. (1997) 'That great supermarket of desire: attributes of the desired other in personal advertisements', in K. Harvey and C. Shalom (eds) *Language and Desire* (Routledge, London).

Smith, D. (1978) 'A peculiar eclipsing: women's exclusion from man's culture', *Women's Studies International Quarterly*, no. 1, pp. 281-96.

Spender, D. (1980) *Man Made Language* (Pandora, London).

Swacker, M. (1975) 'The sex of the speaker as a sociolinguistic variable', in B. Thorne and N. Henley (eds) *Language and Sex: Difference and Dominance* (Newbury House, Rowley, MA).

Tannen, D. (1991) *You Just Don't Understand: Men and Women in Conversation* (Virago, London).

Thorne, B. and Henley, N. (eds) (1975) *Language and Sex: Difference and Dominance* (Newbury House, Rowley, MA).

Trudgill, P. (1980) *Sociolinguistics* (Penguin, Harmondsworth).

US Dept of Labor (1975) *Job Title Revisions*, 3rd edn.

Walker, A. (1983) *The Colour Purple* (The Women's Press, London).

Whorf, B.L. (1956) 'Science and linguistics', in J.B. Carroll (ed.) *Language, Thought and Reality* (MIT Press, Cambridge, MA).

Wilson, T. (1560) *Arte of Rhetorique* (Scolars Facsimiles and Reprints: Gainsville). [Cited in Bodine, A. See full reference above.]

Zimmerman, D. and West, C. (1975) 'Sex roles, interruptions and silences in conversation', in B. Thorne and N. Henley (eds) *Language and Sex: Difference and Dominance* (Newbury House, Rowley, MA).

further reading

All the books in the *Intertext* series, including the core text, cover aspects of language and gender as an integral part of each topic. *The Language of Advertising* and *The Language of Newspapers* both have a strong focus on gender in the language of mass media texts.

If you are interested in exploring further ideas about analysing texts, try
Mills, S. (1995) *Feminist Stylistics* (Routledge, London).

'Political correctness' as an issue can be seen within larger questions about language correctness in general in:
Cameron, D. (1995) *Verbal Hygiene* (Routledge, London).

Cameron, D. (ed.) (1998) *The Feminist Critique of Language* (Routledge, London) and Mills, S. (ed.) (1995) *Language and Gender: Interdisciplinary Perspectives* (Longman, Harlow), both take a good interdisciplinary approach, so that questions about language and gender are related to issues of social and political power. The former text is particularly useful for its historical perspective.

If you are interested in work on how gender, identity and relationships are expressed in everyday popular texts, then look at:
Harvey, K. and Shalom, C. (eds) (1997) *Language and Desire* (Routledge, London).
An older book, but one which still has interesting things to say about gender and popular culture is:
Coward, R. (1984) *Female Desire* (Paladin, London).

If you would like to explore further the extent to which our lives are socially constructed (as opposed to 'natural'), then read:
Burr, V. (1995) *An Introduction to Social Constructionism* (Routledge, London).

The following is a good basic text on language and cognitive processes:
Greene, J. (1986) *Language Understanding: A Cognitive Approach*, Open Guides to Psychology (Oxford University Press, Oxford).

Finally, the following texts offer many interesting ideas on approaches to research, particularly in their treatment of variety and diversity:

Bergvall, V., Bing, J. and Freed, A. (1996) *Rethinking Language and Gender Research* (Longman, Harlow).
Hall, K. and Buchholtz, M. (1995) *Gender Articulated* (Routledge, London).

In Coates, J. and Cameron, D. (eds) (1988) *Women in their Speech Communities* (Longman, Harlow) you can also find further discussion of work done in previous years on sex differences in language, such as ideas about gender and Standard English. This book would therefore support the work you did in Unit five.